Hindu Pilgrimage
The Teerthas

**A journey through the holy places
of Hindus all over India**

by Sunita Pant Bansal

HINDOOLOGY
BOOKS

Published by

HINDOOLOGY
BOOKS

An imprint of

 Pustak Mahal®, **Delhi**

J-3/16 , Daryaganj, New Delhi-110002
☎ 23276539, 23272783, 23272784 • *Fax:* 011-23260518
E-mail: info@pustakmahal.com • *Website:* www.pustakmahal.com

London Office
5, Roddell Court, Bath Road, Slough SL3 OQJ, England
E-mail: pustakmahaluk@pustakmahal.com

Sales Centre
10-B, Netaji Subhash Marg, Daryaganj, New Delhi-110002
☎ 23268292, 23268293, 23279900 • *Fax:* 011-23280567
E-mail: rapidexdelhi@indiatimes.com

Branch Offices
Bangalore: ☎ 22234025
E-mail: pmblr@sancharnet.in • pustak@sancharnet.in
Mumbai: ☎ 22010941
E-mail: rapidex@bom5.vsnl.net.in
Patna: ☎ 3294193 • *Telefax:* 0612-2302719
E-mail: rapidexptn@rediffmail.com
Hyderabad: *Telefax:* 040-24737290
E-mail: pustakmahalhyd@yahoo.co.in

© Copyright : Hindoology Books
ISBN 978-81-223-0997-3

Edition : January 2008

Photo Credits : Devendra Mohan, N.S. Rana and Ajay Lal

Printed in India

Dedicated to

My Grandparents, Parents
&
Ram Avtarji

CONTENTS

TEERTHA

The word teertha comes from 'tri' in Sanskrit, meaning to get rid of all sins, which is a step towards the attainment of final nirvana or moksha. So a place or a person that helps us in getting rid of our sins is considered to be a teertha or a place of pilgrimage.

▲ **A bass relief of holy river Ganga in Mahabalipuram**

According to *Padma Purana*, our teachers *(gurus)* and parents are also *teerthas*, as they provide us with the light of knowledge to cleanse our ignorance and hence lead us on to the right path, towards the *moksha*.

As humans, we lead a life full of struggle and strife. During trying moments, we might knowingly or unknowingly indulge in actions that may be sinful. After a certain time, the wrong actions start weighing us down and our conscience prods us to atone for our sins. That is when we consider visiting a *teertha*, where we can ask for forgiveness. Such a spiritual journey is termed as a pilgrimage or a *teertha yatra*.

According to the *Kashi Khanda* of *Skanda Purana*, the *teerthas* may be divided into three categories — the *Sthawar, Jangam* and *Manas teertha*.

Sthawar teerthas are those places in the Indian subcontinent that have religious or spiritual importance, like the sources of the holy rivers Ganga and Yamuna, mountain peaks like Mount Kailash in the Himalayas, cities like Vrindavan, various forests, *ashrams* etc.

◄ **A sadhu in search of moksha**

Jangam teerthas are the seers, sages and enlightened spiritual masters.

Manas teerthas are our own attributes like truth, forgiveness, kindness, charity, patience and knowledge. They are considered the best of all as they alone help us to purify our inner selves, our character and guide us in the right direction of self-realisation and *moksha*.

Most places of *teerthas* are located in calm and secluded places surrounded by the pristine beauty of nature. We develop spiritual inclination by going to a *teertha*, which purifies us of our material desires.

All desires, material and sensual, lead us away from *moksha*. They entangle us in a vicious web of misery and pain. *Teerthas* provide peace to our otherwise restless soul.

Teerthas have a unifying effect on people. The divisions of caste and creed vanish as we pray with the others. In fact when people of different religious faiths celebrate at a *teertha*, they treat each other as equals, which is the right thing to do. So if we go on a *teertha yatra* often,

▶ Ancient lion sculpture of Mathura

the chances of unrest in the society would lessen. *Teerthas* teach us tolerance towards other people.

The unity in diversity is evident in the major fairs and festivals held at the various *teerthas* across the Indian subcontinent. The Indian art, culture and traditions are best showcased in the Indian *teerthas*. People from all over the world visit India to witness the spiritual enthusiasm, at the time of the *Kumbh Mela*.

▲ Mansarovar Lake

The places of birth of religious and spiritual masters and those where they attained nirvana are also considered as *teerthas*. Some such places in India include Ayodhya, Mathura, Kashi, Gaya etc. The places where one is supposed to conduct the rites of passage, the rituals for birth till death, also fall in the category of *teerthas*.

Kashi, Kailash, Mansarovar are considered **Nitya teerthas** as they are believed to be naturally endowed with spiritual powers since time immemorial. So are the rivers like Ganga, Yamuna, Narmada, Godavari and Kaveri, which are also considered as *Nitya teerthas*.

Places where the gods have descended as *avatar* (incarnation) or have in any way performed miracles are known as **Bhagwadiya teerthas**. Ayodhya, Mathura and Rameshwaram are *Bhagwadiya teerthas*.

The places of birth, enlightenment and penance of the seers and spiritual masters are known as **Sant teerthas**.

This book attempts to take you on a virtual journey to various *teerthas* spread over the length and breadth of India. The *teerthas* are discussed in the book under the categories discussed here.

A sardonyx seal representing Vishnu with a worshipper ▶

◀ Lord Shiva seated with his consort Uma in a 17th century sculpture

1. **ChaarDhaam:** *Chaar* is four and *dhaam* means abode. So *chaar dhaam* are four abodes or dwelling places of God. According to our scriptures, Lord Vishnu descended in the east at Jagannath Puri, in the west at Dwarka, in the north at Badrinath and in the south at Rameshwaram. Hence these sacred places are together known as *chaar dhaam*.

2. **Himalayan Chaar Dhaam:** Apart from these, the Indian State of Uttarakhand also has Himalayan *chaar dhaam*, which are Yamunotri, Gangotri, Kedarnath and Badrinath. It is believed that the pilgrimage to Himalayan *chaar dhaam* absolves you of all the sins of your past.

3. **Sapt Puri:** The seven holy cities *(puri)* are Ayodhya, Mathura, Haridwar, Varanasi, Kanchipuram, Ujjain and Dwarka.

4. **Dwadash Jyotirlingam:** There are twelve *lingams* of Lord Shiva in India. They are known as *dwadash jyotirlingams*. They are located at Somnath, Mallikarjuna, Mahakaleshwar, Baidyanath, Omkareshwar, Bhimshankar, Nageshwar, Kashi-Vishwanath, Triambakeshwar, Kedarnath, Rameshwar and Ghrishneshwar.

5. **Panch Sarovar:** These are the five holy lakes in India where taking a dip washes away your sins. They are Mansarovar, Pushkar, Bindu Sarovar, Narayan Sarovar and Pampa.

6. **Sapt Sarita:** Though the *Vedas* and *Puranas* mention more, but seven Indian rivers are considered the most sacred ones in the country. They are Ganga, Yamuna, Godavari, Saraswati, Narmada, Sindhu and Kaveri. There are many temples on the banks of these rivers where people can go and pray to cleanse their sins.

7. **Divya Desams:** There are one hundred and eight *Divya Desam* temples of Lord Vishnu. It is said that Alwars (saint poets) sang their verses at these places.

8. **Shakti Peetha:** There are fifty-one *Shakti Peethas* of *Devi* (Goddess) throughout the country.

9. **Yatras:** These are the spiritual journeys which the pilgrims undertake to a special *teertha*. Some of the famous *yatras* include Kailash-Mansarovar Yatra, Amarnath Yatra, Panch Kedar Yatra, Vaishno Devi Yatra, Sabarimala Yatra and Alandi-Pandharpur Yatra.

10. **Some Other Famous Temples:** These include the seven Sun Temples and five other famous temples.

▲ **An ancient coin showing Lord Varaha, a Vishnu avatar**

CHAAR DHAAM

Dhaam means abode of God — a place where God resides.

There are four houses (dhaam) of God, in the four corners of India. These are Badrinath in the north, Jagannath Puri in the east, Rameshwaram in the south and Dwarka in the west. Pious Hindus visit these four holy places for salvation.

1. Badrinath ▶

Badrinath is at an elevation of 3100 metres, on a plateau between Narayana Parbat and the Alaknanda River in the region of Garhwal Himalayas in Uttarakhand. The Nara and Narayana peaks tower over the shrine, which is located 301 kilometres north of Rishikesh. It is one of the eight self-manifested holy *teerthas* in India.

◀ ## 2. Jagannath Puri

Puri is located 60 kilometres from Bhubaneswar in Orissa on the coast of the Bay of Bengal. The Jagannath Temple here is one of the most famous temples in India.

3. Dwarka

Dwarka was Lord Krishna's capital 5000 years ago, after he left Mathura. Lord Krishna spent 100 years here. Modern day Dwarka is a small city located at the western tip of the Gujarat peninsula on the Arabian Sea.

4. Rameshwaram

Rameshwaram is located at the south-eastern end of the Indian Peninsula in the State of Tamil Nadu. Rameshwaram is on a conch-shaped island in the Gulf of Mannar.

BADRINATH

Badrinath is the abode of Lord Vishnu as Badri Narayana. Badrinath is considered as one of the most sacred centres of pilgrimage situated in the lofty Himalayan heights in the Tehri-Garhwal hill tracks in Uttarakhand.

◀ **The facade of Badrinath Temple**

Badrinath Temple

The statue of Lord Badrinath is self-manifested from a 2-foot-high black *shaligram-shila* (rock). It is also known as Badri Vishal or Badri Narayana. The details of the statue are not very distinct due to weathering, since it was thrown into Narada Kund and remained there for several years during the Buddhist period. Lord Badri Narayana is said to have been installed by Shankaracharya, who recovered the deity from the Kund.

Lord Badrinath is sitting meditating in the *padmasana* (lotus posture). Standing to his right side is Uddhava. To the far right side are Nara and Narayana. Narada Muni is kneeling in front on the right side. On the left side are Kuber, the God of wealth, and Ganesha. Garuda is kneeling in front, to the left of Badri Narayana.

The canopy over the deities is covered with a sheet of pure gold. The temple is full of ancient stone carvings. Within the temple enclosure, to the left of the main temple building is a separate shrine dedicated to Lakshmi Devi and the *gaddi* (sitting place) of Adi Shankaracharya, just outside the exit door of the temple. Near the temple are a number of *kunds* or tanks filled with hot sulphur water. Pilgrims bathe here before entering the shrine.

The temple is open for six months of the year, May to October. For the rest of the year, the priests of the temple perform their *puja* (worship) in Joshimath. Before they close the temple in November, the priests perform one last *puja* and leave the *ghee diyas* (lamps) in the temple lit. Six months later, in the month of May they return to open the temple and find the lamps still lit. It is believed that Narada Muni carries on the worship during those months, as it was here where he had attained salvation.

▲ **Lord Badri Narayana**

Narada Kund is a few feet away from the Alaknanda River on the side of the temple.

Panch Shilas named as Narada, Narasimha, Varaha, Garuda and Markendeya are located by Tapta Kund. These are the five large rocks near the river.

The two mountains by the name of Nara Parbat and Narayana Parbat are also here. Nara Parbat is located just opposite the main temple and Narayana Parbat is behind it. They are named after Nara and Narayana Rishis who did meditation here. Neelkantha Peak (6,596 metres) is to the left of Narayana Parbat.

Panch Dhara is the confluence of five waterfalls — Kurma, Prahlada, Urvashi, Bhrigu and Indra, which are all located around Badrinath.

Near **Keshava Prayag**, there is a temple dedicated to the mother of Nara and Narayana Rishis. Near this temple is a mountain called **Maninag Parbat** where it is believed that Yudhishthira was able to answer all the questions asked by a *yaksha* to bring his brothers back to life. They had lost their lives when they could not answer the questions.

Mana village is 4 kilometres north-west of Badrinath towards the Tibet border. **Vyas Gufa** is the famous cave located here where Ved Vyas is believed to have written the four *Vedas*.

Nearby is **Ganesha's Cave**. It was around here that Lord Shiva narrated the glories of the Himalayas to sage Skanda, who wrote the *Skanda Purana*.

Down below is the bridge named **Bhima Pul**, which Bhima is said to have made from a huge stone slab so that his brothers and Draupadi could cross the Saraswati River safely. The Saraswati River emerges from a glacier located in the north of Mana, touches Vyas Gufa, merges into the Alakananda at Keshava Prayag and finally meets the Ganga and Yamuna in Allahabad.

▼   **Badrinath, the adobe of Lord Vishnu**

Satopanth Lake is a glacial lake 25 kilometres from Badrinath. It is believed that Lord Brahma, Lord Vishnu and Lord Shiva meditated at the three corners of this lake.

Four Badris

There are four more Badri temples — Adi Badri, Vriddha Badri, Bhavishya Badri and Yogadhyan Badri.

Adi Badri is 18 kilometres south from Karna Prayag towards Gwaldam. The main temple comprises a three-foot carved black stone statue of Lord Adi Badri Narayana. He holds a mace, *chakra* and lotus.

Vriddh Badri is on the way to Pipalkoti. When Narada performed *tapasya* here, Lord Vishnu appeared before him as *vriddha* (old) Badri.

Bhavishya Badri is 24 kilometres from Joshimath.

Yogadhyan Badri is the place where King Pandu, the father of Pandavas, performed penance to atone for the curse he received for killing two mating deer, who were sages in their previous lives. It is said that the Pandavas were born here and King Pandu installed a bronze statue of Lord Vishnu, which came to be known as Yogadhyan Badri.

When Badrinath closes during the winter, the priests from the Badrinath Temple come to **Joshimath** and continue to worship at the Narasimha Temple. Also there is an ancient Vasudeva Temple, dedicated to Lord Krishna, in Joshimath.

Narasimha Temple has an idol of Lord Narasimha, which is self-manifested from a *shaligram-shila*. It is about 10 inches high and remarkably detailed, sitting in a lotus position. To the right of Lord Narasimha are Sita, Rama, Hanuman and Garuda. Against the left wall is an idol of Chandika, which is another name for Kali. On the altar to the right of Lord Narasimha are the statues of Kubera, Uddhava, and Badri Vishal. There is an altar for

▲ Badrinath Puri

Goddess Lakshmi just outside the door of the temple. This temple is over 1200 years old.

Vasudeva Temple is one of the 108 *Divya Desams*. The black carved stone statue of Lord Vasudeva is about 6 feet tall. This temple is about 30 yards from the Narasimha Temple. To the left of the main entrance is the rare idol of dancing Ganesha. This temple is very ancient, and no one knows exactly how old it is.

Vishnu Prayag is 10 kilometres past Joshimath. Alakananda and Dhauli Ganga join together at Vishnu Prayag. 10 kilometres further is Govind Ghat, which is where the treks to the Valley of Flowers and Sri Hemkund Sahib begin.

Pandukeshwara is 4 kilometres further up the road. This town is the site of the Yogadhyan Badri Temple where the statue of Badri Vishal is brought from Badrinath during the six winter months when the Badrinath temple closes from November to May.

Shankaracharya Math

▼ Adi Badri

This is a temple located on the ridge above the upper part of the town. If you enter the temple and follow the

▼ The holy town of Badrinath

signs to your left, you come to the cave where Shankaracharya is said to have meditated. If you go up the stairs to the right of the temple entrance, you come to the *Kalpavriksha* tree, where Shankaracharya attained self-realisation.

Hanuman Chatti

It is 9 kilometres further up the road. It is said that Bhima and Hanuman tested each other's strength in the Gandhmadana Hills and realised that they were both sons of Vayu and therefore brothers. According to the legend, Bhima was travelling, when he came across an old monkey lying in his way. Bhima requested the monkey to move his tail that was blocking his way. The monkey replied that he was very old and had no strength, so Bhima could try to move it himself. After repeated attempts to move the tail, the powerful Bhima gave up. The monkey then revealed himself as Hanuman.

Valley of Flowers

The beautiful Valley of Flowers, 5 kilometres from Ghangaria, gets all covered with a large variety of flowers after the rainy season i.e. between June and September The valley is about 10 kilometres long and 2 kilometres wide.

Lake Hemkund

From Ghangaria, following the Lakshman Ganga, you reach Lake Hemkund. In the Granth Sahib, the tenth Sikh Guru Gobind Singh has written that in his previous life, he meditated on the shore of a lake that was surrounded by seven snow-capped mountains. The bank of Hemkund Lake is accepted as this place. There is a large Gurudwara and a small Lakshman temple at this place. As per the Ramayana, Lakshman meditated by the lake and regained his health here after he was seriously wounded by Meghnad, the son of Ravana.

JAGANNATH PURI

While several ancient temples have vanished or ruined with the passage of time, the great temple of Lord Jagannath at Puri is still a living and vibrant temple. Ever since the pre-historic times, it has attracted kings, conquerors, spiritual leaders, devotees and pilgrims. In the minds of the millions of Indians, Orissa holds a special place as the land of Jagannath, the Lord of the Universe. This temple of Lord Jagannath at Puri is one of the most sacred pilgrimage spots in India.

Jagannath Temple

Jagannath literally means the Lord of the Universe. The construction of this temple is believed to be started by King Chora Ganga Deva and completed by his descendant, Anangabhima Deva, in the 12th century. The main temple structure is 65 metres high and is built on elevated ground, which makes it look even larger. The temple complex comprises an area of about 11 acres and is enclosed by two rectangular walls. The outer enclosure is called **Meghanada Prachira**, while the inner wall is known as **Kurmabedha**. The walls were built during the 15th or 16th century.

There is a wheel on top of the Jagannath temple made of an alloy of eight different metals known as *ashta dhatu*. It is known as *Neela Chakra* (the blue wheel). The main temple is surrounded by thirty different smaller temples.

The **Narasimha Temple**, adjacent to the western side of the Mukti mandapa, was constructed before the present temple. The main deities in the temple are Lord Jagannath, his brother Baladeva, and his sister Subhadra. Jagannath is another name for Lord Krishna.

Next to the main temple is the hall of audience, which one can enter through four separate doors. The **Kalaghata door** leads to the sanctum sanctorum. The southern door leads out of the temple and the northern to the *Ratna bhandar* (the treasury).

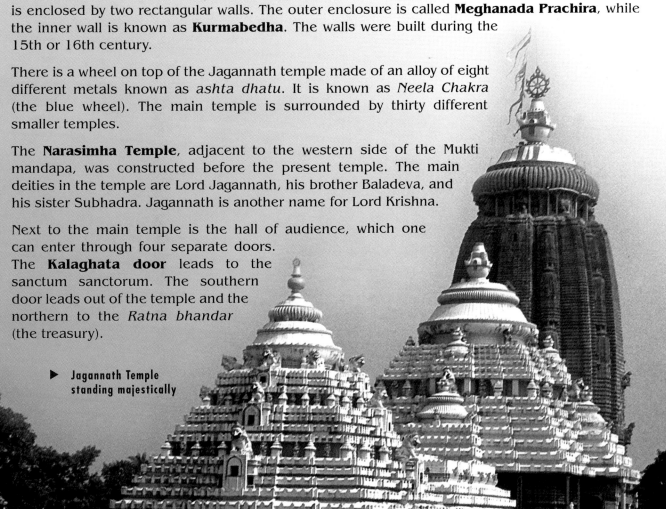

▶ Jagannath Temple standing majestically

Nata Mandir is a spacious hall. This is where the **Garuda Stambha** is located, where Lord Chaitanya used to stand. **Bhoga Mandap** is a hall next to Nata Mandira.

There are sculptures and paintings in this hall that narrate the stories of Lord Krishna. In front of the main gate is an 11-metre-tall pillar, called **Aruna Stambha**, which used to be in front of the Sun Temple in Konark. It was brought to Puri during the 18th century. The figure on top of the pillar is of *Aruna*, the charioteer of the Sun-god. In the passage room of this gate is an idol of Lord Jagannath called *Patita Pavana* (saviour of the fallen). This idol is visible from the road, which facilitates even the passers-by to take *darshan* of the Lord.

There are four gates, the eastern *Singhadwar* (lion gate), the southern *Ashwadwar* (horse gate), the western *Vyaghradwar* (tiger gate), and the northern *Hastidwar* (elephant gate). There is a carving of each form by the entrance of each gate.

Nearby Places

Gundicha Temple is located at the end of the Grand Road about 3 kilometres north-east of the Jagannath Temple. The legends say that at the time of the Ratha Yatra festival, Lord Jagannath goes to the Gundicha Temple and stays there for one week. After one week, he returns to his original temple. Gundicha was the wife of Indradyumna, the king who originally established the temple of Jagannath.

Narasimha Temple is a well-constructed spectacular temple. There are two deities of Lord

▲ **The celebrated Ratha Yatra**

▲ **The statue of Ugra Narasimha**

Narasimha in the temple, one behind the other. The deity in front is called Sant Narasimha, calm-looking, devoid of any anger, frustration or anxiety.

The deity in the back is called Raga Narasimha, angry-looking, depicting the internal mood of Narasimha.

Jagannath Vallabha Temple was used by Ramananda Raya to train girls in dancing for the pleasure of Lord Jagannath. There are three altars in the temple. On one altar, there are large statues of Lord Jagannath, Baladeva, and Subhadra. On the middle altar, there are deities of Lord Chaitanya (in saffron) and Ramananda Raya (in white). On the third altar are the statues of Radha and Krishna. This place is about 1 kilometre from the Jagannath Temple.

Tota Gopinath Temple houses the deity of Tota Gopinath. It is believed that Sri Chaitanya Mahaprabhu ended his manifested pastimes in Jagannath Puri by entering into the knee of the Tota Gopinath deity. In the temple, on the left altar are Lord Balarama and his two wives, Revati and Varuni. On the middle altar is Tota Gopinath accompanied by black deities of Radha and Lalita. Tota Gopinath is in a sitting position. On the right altar are the deities of Radha-Madanmohan and Gaura-Gadadhar. This temple is located in the Gaurbat Sahi area. It is a five-minute-walk from the Chatak Parbat Purushottam Gaudiya Math Temple.

Chatak Parbat Gaudiya Math Temple is in the area where Sri Chaitanya mistook the sand dune hills to be the Govardhan Hill. **Narendra Sarovar** is a large tank located off Grand Road, on the same side as the Jagannath Temple.

This small temple is on an island about a 100 feet into the sarovar, with deities of Lord Jagannath, Baladeva, and Subhadra. Directly behind Lord Jagannath is a statue of Yashoda, the mother of Krishna. At the other end of the temple is a statue of Lakshmi. Also on the island are Shiva Temple and an idol of Bala Krishna.

Balagandhi is the place where Lord Jagannath stops his chariot to accept a massive *bhoga* (offering). There is a temple on the right side of the main road marking the spot, about a kilometre down from the Lion Gate on the way to Gundicha Temple. Alalanatha is also known as Brahmagiri. It is about 25 kilometres from Jagannath Puri, close to the beach. There is a temple of Lord Jagannath here and a large stone slab marked with the impression of Sri Chaitanya's transcendental body. There is a stone here which was believed to have melted when he lay on it in ecstasy. At the rear of the temple is a sculpture of Narasimha, with Hiranyakashipu in his lap. There is also a sculpture of Lord Vamana piercing the outer shell of the Universe.

Atharanala Bridge is at the entrance of Puri. It has eighteen arches *Athara* means eighteen. The present bridge is an addition, constructed directly on top of the original brick bridge. You can also see the temple *chakra* from it.

Ratha Yatra

During this festival, the deities of Lord Jagannath, Baladeva, and Subhadra are carried out of the temple.

▲ **Market near the Temple**

▲ **Streets flooded with pilgrims**

This famous festival begins from the second day of the bright fortnight of *Ashadha* during the month of June/July. The chariot of Lord Jagannath is known as **Nandighosh**. It is 14 metres high and has eighteen wheels. It is covered with yellow and red cloth and a chakra rests on top of the chariot.

The chariot of Baladeva is 13 metres high and has sixteen wheels. It is called **Taladhwaja** and the cloth on the roof is red and green. It is crowned with a Tala fruit.

Subhadra's cart is 12 metres high and has fourteen wheels. It is named **Padmadhwaja** and is covered with red and black cloth. There are side deities on each of the chariots.

With the exception of the *kalasha* (the pinnacles on top of the chariots), the side deities, the wooden charioteers and horses which are all reused, the chariots are constructed afresh each year.

Chandana Yatra

Chandana Yatra takes place in the month of April. During this *yatra*, the processional deities are taken for a boat ride in the Narendra Sarovar after they are bathed in sandalwood *(chandana)* scented water. The festival lasts for forty-two days.

Snana Yatra

Snana Yatra is when the main deities are bathed with 108 pots of water on *Jyestha Purnima*. This is done before the celebration of Ratha Yatra.

DWARKA

Dwarka is the abode of Lord Krishna as Dwarkadhish. It is one of the **Sapt Puri** *or seven holy cities of India, which include Ayodhya, Mathura, Haridwar, Kashi (Varanasi), Avantika (Ujjain) and Kanchipuram.*

Ancient Dwarka

Srimad Bhagavatam describes Dwarka of 5000 years ago, when Narada came to visit Lord Krishna. As Narada arrived in Dwarka, he saw that the gardens and parks were full of various flowers of different colours and the orchards were overloaded with variety of fruits.

In this greatly beautiful city of Dwarka, Lord Krishna had 16,000 palaces, built by Vishvakarma, the engineer of the gods. A different queen of Lord Krishna resided in each of them. The pillars of the palaces were made of corals and the ceilings were adorned with jewels. The walls as well as the arches between the pillars glowed from the decorations of different kinds of sapphires. Throughout the palaces, the canopies were decorated with strings of pearls. The chairs and other furniture were made of ivory, ornamented with gold and diamonds and jewelled lamps dissipated the darkness within the palace. It is believed that after Krishna ended his earthly journey, the sea claimed his Dwarka, sparing only Krishna's home where Dwarkadhish Temple stands today.

Bet Dwarka

Bet Dwarka or Dwarka Island is located 30 kilometres north of Dwarka on an island in the middle of the Arabian Sea, next to the coastal town of Okha. It is a twenty-minute boat ride to the island. Bet Dwarka is said to be the remains of the original city of Dwarka and here is where Lord Krishna's childhood friend Sudama came to meet him. Apart from Dwarkadhish Temple, there is also a Balarama (dauji) Temple here.

◀ **Dwarkadhish Temple, the abode of Lord Krishna**

Dwarkadhish Temple

In the middle of the town is the Dwarkadhish Temple which was built in the 16th century. Dwarkadhish is another name of Lord Krishna. It means the Lord of Dwarka. The five-storey-high temple is built on seventy-two pillars. Lord Krishna's grandson, Vajranabha, is believed to have built the original temple of Dwarkadhish over the Harigriha, Lord Krishna's residential palace.

The sanctum of the temple is formed by the **Jagat Mandir** or **Nija Mandir**, which dates back 2500 years. The Jagat Mandir has a tall tower and a hall of audience. There are two entrances to the temple. The main entrance (north entrance) is called *Moksha Dwar* (door to salvation). The south entrance is called *Swarga Dwar* (door to heaven).

The main deity in this temple is Lord Dwarkadhish, who is on the central altar. The deity represents the four-armed form of Vishnu called Trivikrama. There is a temple on the right that contains the deity of Lord Balarama, the elder brother of Lord Krishna.

The temple to the left contains deities of Pradyumna and Aniruddha. They were respectively the son and grandson of Lord Krishna.

Opposite this place is the shrine of Purushottama (Vishnu). Next to this is a shrine dedicated to Kusheshwara Mahadeva (Shiva).

The shrine that is across from Lord Dwarkadhish contains the deity of Devaki, the mother of Lord Krishna. Next to this shrine is a temple dedicated to Radha, Jambavati, Satyabhama and Lakshmi.

Rukmini Devi Temple is 1.5 kilometres north of the town. It is an architectural masterpiece. Rukmini was the most loved one of Krishna's 16,108 wives. The temple

▲ **Lord Dwarkadhish**

walls are decorated with beautiful paintings depicting the pastimes of Rukmini and Krishna. This temple dates back to the 12th century.

The legend says that Rishi Durvasa had once invited Lord Krishna and his wife Rukmini to dinner. The etiquette is that a person invited for dinner, should not eat or drink unless served by his host. Now Rukmini became very thirsty and asked Krishna to help. Krishna quietly pushed his toe in the ground and the water came forth. But as Rukmini was drinking water, Durvasa saw her. He became very angry and cursed her to live in separation from Lord Krishna. That is why Krishna's temple is in the town and her temple is located on the outskirts.

▲ **The sacred Gomati Ghat**

Gomati Ghat Temples

The **Dwarkadhish Temple** is located almost at the spot where River Gomati meets the ocean. Gomati meets the sea at Chakra Tirtha Ghat. To take a bath where the Gomati meets the ocean is supposed to give liberation to a devotee.

There is **Samudra Narayana Temple** (Sangam Narayana) at the confluence of the Gomati River and the sea.

At **Chakra Narayana**, Lord Vishnu manifested himself as a stone marked with a chakra on the seashore.

The **Gomatiji Temple** has an image of the Gomati River which is believed to have been brought down from the heaven by Sage Vashishtha.

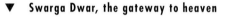

▼ Swarga Dwar, the gateway to heaven

▲ Nageshwar Mahadev Temple

Nageshwar Mahadev Temple contains one of the 12 Shiva Jyotirlingams in an underground sanctum. It is located 17 kilometres from Dwarka.

Mul Dwarkadhish is 25 kilometres north of Porbandar on the way to Dwarka. Located here are the Mul Dwarkadhish temple and a well that is said to be as sacred as the Ganges. As per the myth, Lord Krishna stopped here on his way to Dwarka.

Gopi Talava, 23 kilometres north of Dwarka, is where Lord Krishna met the *gopis* when they came to see him. This sacred kund was their meeting place, and the sacred soil here is known as *gopi chandana*, used by devotees for *tilak.*

RAMESHWARAM

Rameshwaram is located at the south-eastern end of Indian Peninsula. It is on a conch-shaped island. The island is sanctified by the footprints of Lord Rama. The legends say that Lord Rama bathed at Dhanushkodi, where the Bay of Bengal and the Indian Ocean meet. Right next to the sea is a magnificent Lord Shiva Temple known as the Ramanathaswamy Temple.

Sri Ramanathaswamy Temple

This is one of the major Lord Shiva Temples in India. Parts of the present temple were built in the 12th century. The temple covers a 15-acre-area. The eastern *gopuram* (gate) is 53 metres high. The temple is about 200 metres from the sea, facing east. Non-Hindus are not allowed to enter the inner sanctum. The sea at *Agni Teertham*, about 200 metres from the temple, is a sacred bathing place. It is said that if you take a bath here, all your sins are washed away. It is a tradition to take a bath at *Agni Teertham* before entering the Ramanathaswamy Temple.

It is said that the Shivalingam in Ramanathaswamy Temple was installed by Sri Rama on his return to the main land from the island of Lanka, in order to absolve himself of the sin of killing Ravana, who was a Brahmin. Rama sent Hanuman to Mount Kailash to get the *lingam*.

Since Hanuman was late, when the auspicious time for installation neared, Sita made a Shivalingam out of sand, which was installed by Rama and is known as the Ramalingam. When Hanuman came with Shivalingam from Kailash, he was disappointed. Rama told Hanuman that he could replace the *lingam* made by Sita with the one brought by him. Hanuman tried pulling the *lingam* first with his hands and then by wrapping his tail around it, but could not move it.

To pacify Hanuman, Rama had the *lingam* (which came to be known as Vishwalingam) that he brought installed alongside the Ramalingam and ordered that *puja* (worship) be first offered to the Vishwalingam.

As you enter the main eastern entrance, there is a deity of Hanuman trying to uproot the Ramalingam. There is a 1220-metre-long

▶ **Front gopuram of**
Sri Ramanathaswamy Temple

beautiful corridor which goes around the temple, with large sculptured pillars that are elaborately deigned and carved. It is the longest temple corridor in India. The corridor is 9 metres high and 6 metres wide. If you proceed straight, you come to the huge Nandi bull (carrier of Lord Shiva) and then you come to the Ramanathaswamy Shiva shrine.

▲ Dhanushkodi beach near Rameshwaram

In the principal sanctum is the *lingam* of Sri Ramanatha. This is the *lingam* that Sita made and Sri Rama sanctified. The Vishwalingam, installed by Hanuman, is to the right of the Ramalingam, on an altar along the north wall. Worship is first offered to this lingam. The shrine of Goddess Parvati, the consort of Lord Shiva, is to the left of the Ramalingam.

There are 22 *teerthams* or bathing tanks in the temple in which pilgrims traditionally bathe before seeing the deities. Each tank is said to give a different benefit, hence many pilgrims bathe in all the 22 tanks before seeing the deities.

Other Places

Gandhamadan Parbat is a two-storeyed temple on a small hilltop about 2.5 kilometres north-west of the Ramanathaswamy Temple. There is a set of Lord Rama's footprints on a *chakra*. There is a small Ramajharokha Temple here. Hanuman is said to have made his great leap to Lanka from here.

Kothandaramaswamy Temple has deities of Sri Rama, Sita, Lakshman, Hanuman, and Vibhishana. It is said that Vibhishana, Ravana's brother, surrendered to Lord Rama at this place. The story is depicted through a series of paintings inside the temple. In 1964, a cyclone wiped out everything in the surrounding area. The only thing left standing was this temple which is located about 8 kilometres from Rameshwaram.

Dhanushkodi is the place where the Bay meets the ocean at about 20 kilometres south-east of Rameshwaram. Pilgrims bathe in the small lagoon here called Ratnakara.

◀ A sadhu praying at Rameshwaram Beach

▲ **Through the corridor of sanctity**

When Lord Rama went to Lanka with the monkey army, they crossed the ocean on a bridge of floating rocks. It is said that Lord Rama destroyed the stone bridge with his bow before returning to Ayodhya at the request of Vibhishana, the younger brother of Ravana.

There is a temple nearby where floating rocks can be found. Near this temple are *Lakshman Teertham* and *Rama Teertham*. Rama and Lakshman are believed to have bathed in these two tanks.

Kodi Teertham is the spring that Lord Rama created by shooting an arrow into the ground.

At *Jata Teertham*, Rama washed his hair to get rid of any sins that he might have incurred in the battle at Lanka.

▲ **Agni teertham**

HIMALAYAN CHAAR DHAAM

*Apart from these, the Indian state of Uttarakhand also has **Chaar Dhaam**, which comprises **Yamunotri, Gangotri, Kedarnath** and **Badrinath**. They are located in the Himalayan region.*

1. Yamunotri

Yamumotri stands on the western flank of the forever snow-covered Bandarpoonch Mountain at a height of 6315 metres. Yamunotri is the source of Hanuman Ganga and Tons River which are the tributaries of Yamuna.

2. Gangotri

Gangotri is located about 250 kilometres from Rishikesh and 230 kilometres from Yamunotri. Gangotri is at an elevation of 3140 metres. The actual source of the Ganga is Gaumukh, a 19-kilometre-climb from Gangotri.

3. Kedarnath

Kedarnath is on the bank of the Mandakini River between Gangotri and Badrinath.

4. Badrinath

Badrinath is 42 kilometres from Kedarnath. We have already discussed it in the section on *Chaar Dhaam*.

Tradition is that the pilgrims visit Yamunotri and Gangotri first and bring with them the holy waters from the sources of the rivers Yamuna and Ganga. Thereafter they offer *abhishekams* to Kedareshwara and Badri Narayana.

▲ The regal Himalayas

YAMUNOTRI

The holy Yamuna River originates from Yamunotri. Yamunotri is about 234 kilometres north of Haridwar. The Yamuna flows west to east at Yamunotri.

*Yamunotri is near a hot spring at the foothill of Kalinda Parbat. The climb from Hanuman Chatti, where the road ends, takes five to six hours. On the way up is the confluence of the Yamuna and Neel Ganga, called **Shani Prayag**. There is a temple here dedicated to Shani.*

▲ **Yamunotri, the birthplace of Yamuna**

Saptarishi Kund

The actual source of the Yamuna is located at Saptarishi Kund. To reach there, you must have a guide. It is believed that seven great sages, Rishi Kashyap, Atri, Bhardwaj, Vishwamitra, Gautama, Jamadagni and Vashishtha performed austerities for millions of years here. The kund is about a half kilometre in diameter, and its water is dark blue with slushy snow. Very few people go there as it is a difficult place to reach.

Yamunotri Temple

The Yamunotri Temple is built at the base of Kalinda Parbat. The temple is dedicated to the goddess Yamuna. The deity of Yamuna is carved from black stone, and there is also a deity of Ganga Devi, which is white. Yamuna is said to be the daughter of Surya (the Sun God) and the sister of Yamaraja, the God of Death.

Close to the temple are some hot water springs where the water gushes out at boiling point. At **Surya Kund**, which is perhaps the most sacred one, pilgrims wrap rice and potatoes in a cloth and place it in the hot water. Within a few minutes, the rice and potatoes get cooked. Right next to the temple is **Divya Shila**, which is worshipped before *puja* is offered to Yamunaji.

Hanuman Chatti

It takes five to six hours to walk uphill from Hanuman Chatti to Yamunotri. At a distance of 6.4 kilometres from Hanuman Chatti, there are sulphur springs. It is a steep and continuous climb to the top, just wide enough for two horses to pass. If you cannot walk up the hill, you may opt for a *dandi*, which is like a palanquin carried by four persons. It is the most comfortable means of transportation here. Pony or horse rides are also offered, but they may be uncomfortable for some people.

▼ **Yamunotri Temple**

GANGOTRI

King Bhagiratha is said to have prayed at Gangotri to bring Ganga down from the heaven to salvage his ancestors. The Pandavas are also said to have visited this place to atone for the sin of killing their relatives during the Kurukshetra war. At this point the Ganga River flowed north, giving this place its name, Gangotri, which means 'Ganga turned north'.

At Gangotri, the Kedar Ganga merges with the Bhagirathi. There is a waterfall called Sahasradhara near this confluence. Just before the falls, the river squeezes itself into a narrow gorge about 1 metre wide.

▼ **Gangotri Temple**

▲ The revered shrine of Gangotri

Gangotri Temple

The Gangotri Temple is dedicated to the goddess Ganga. It is erected near a sacred stone called Bhagiratha Shila which is about 50 feet to the left of the temple. King Bhagiratha is said to have sat here to worship, so that Lord Shiva would take the Ganga on his head. Soon after *arati* to all the deities in the temple, an *arati* is performed to the holy River Ganga.

The legend goes that during Satyuga, King Sagar performed a horse sacrifice *(Ashvamedha Yajna)* to prove his supremacy. Lord Indra became fearful over the possible results of the *yajna*, so he stole the horse and left it at the ashram of Kapila Muni, who was in deep meditation. King Sagar's 60,000 sons, born of Queen Sumati, and his son Asmanjas, born of Queen Kesoni, were then sent to find the horse. When the sons found the horse at Kapila Muni's ashram, they thought he had stolen it and they prepared to attack the meditating sage. Kapila Muni's meditation was disturbed. He opened his eyes and burned Sagar's 60,000 sons to ashes. Asmanjas was not burned and returned to tell the story to King Sagar, who then sent his grandson Anshuman to get the horse back. Kapila Muni returned the horse and told the king that his sons were burnt because they disturbed his meditation. He said his sons could attain salvation only if goddess Ganga descended to earth and bathed their ashes in her waters.

King Sagar's great grandson, Bhagiratha, eventually pleased goddess Ganga and requested her to come down to the earth. But the force of the Ganga coming from heaven would have been too great for the earth to handle, so she needed someone to buffer the fall. After being worshipped by Bhagiratha, Lord Shiva agreed to bear the powerful force of the descending river on his head. King Bhagiratha then preceded the holy river, which followed him to Ganga Sagar at the Bay of Bengal. The Ganga then bathed the remains of the 60,000 sons of King Sagar and thus helped them to return to their eternal positions.

Gaumukh

This glacier is the actual source of the Ganga. Gaumukh means a cow's face, which the glacier looks like. It has a rocky path, marked white on one side. The water of the Bhagirathi gushes out from the glacier with great force and cuts a fantastic gorge out of the mountains. The climb is difficult and treacherous.

There is a flight of stairs by the Gangotri Temple that leads to the path that goes to Gaumukh.

Tapovan

Past Gaumukh, 5 kilometres away, is Tapovan. It is near a natural Shivalingam peak. It is called Tapovan because *sadhus* performed *tapasya* (penance) here to attain nirvana (salvation).

Kedar Tal

It is the source of Kedar Ganga, a 17-kilometre-trek from Gangotri. The trek starts at Dev Ghat in Gangotri, following Kedar Ganga up for 8 kilometres till Bhoj Kharak, then another 4 kilometres to Kedar Kharak and finally another 5 kilometres to Kedar Tal. Bhrigupanth and Thalesagar are the two important mountains here.

▲ The holy bells in the temple

Guptakashi

The Pandavas went to Kashi (Varanasi) to get Lord Shiva's blessings, but Lord Shiva fled to Guptakashi and lived incognito. Eventually, the Pandavas found him, but Lord Shiva then turned himself to a bull to hide from them. Because Lord Shiva was hiding here, the place was given the name Guptakashi.

Guptakashi has two main temples dedicated to **Ardhanareshwara** (Gaurishankar) and **Vishwanath**. In front of the Vishwanath Temple is a small kund (tank) called **Manikarnika**. Water from a Ganesha head and from a cow's head flows into the kund. Water from one is called the Ganga and water from the other is called the Yamuna. It is believed that this water comes from Gangotri and Yamunotri. Guptakashi is 45 kilometres south of Kedarnath.

The town of **Agastya Muni**, 25 kilometres before Guptakashi, is where Agastya Muni meditated. There is an **Agastya Temple** here.

Triyugi Narayana

Triyugi Narayana is located between Gangotri and Kedarnath. Triyugi Narayana is about 5 kilometres off the main road and can be reached from Sitapur or Son Prayag. It is said that the marriage of Lord Shiva and Parvati took place here at **Brahma Shila**. Brahma was the priest who conducted the marriage and Lord Narayana offered his sister Parvati to Lord Shiva. It is believed that the marriage

▲ Ganga, on its circuitous course

havan kund has been burning since that time. Pilgrims offer samidha (pieces of wood) in the havan kund and take the ashes as prasada. It is said that the present **Akhand Dhuni Temple** was built by Adi Shankaracharya 1200 years ago. In this temple, there is a 2-foot-high silver deity of Lord Narayana (Vishnu) with Lakshmi and Saraswati on either side. There is a stone outside the temple that marks the spot where the marriage was performed and also the four holy kunds called Vishnu Kund, Brahma Kund, Rudra Kund and Saraswati Kund.

▲ The snow-clad Gangotri Valley

KEDARNATH

Kedarnath is only 42 kilometres from Badrinath. It is believed that Shankaracharya attained samadhi here. Kedareshwara is the presiding deity at the Kedarnath Temple.

Kedarnath Temple

This Lord Shiva temple at Kedarnath is said to have been originally built by the Pandavas to cleanse their sins that they incurred during the Kurukshetra war. The temple is dedicated to Lord Shiva and is considered to be one of the major Shiva temples in India.

The legend of the temple is that the Pandavas asked Lord Shiva for his blessings to relieve them from the sinful act of the Kurukshetra war. The Pandavas first went to Kashi (Varanasi) to get Lord Shiva's blessings but the Lord fled to Guptakashi and lived there in disguise. Eventually the Pandavas found him there but Lord Shiva turned himself into a bull. Bhima recognised his disguise and grabbed the bull by the tail. The bull sank into the ground and Lord Shiva appeared. Lord Shiva instructed the Pandavas to worship the hump *(pinda)* of the bull. A temple was then constructed and worship has been going on here ever since. Other parts of Lord Shiva's body appeared in other places in the area.

It is said that the Pandavas also built temples at these places. They are known as the Panch Kedars — Kedarnath for hump *(pinda)*, Tungnath for arm *(bahu)*, Rudranath for face *(mukh)*, Kalpeshwara for hair *(jata)* and Madhyamaheshwara for navel *(nabhi)*.

◀ **Kedarnath Temple**

Gauri Kund

Gauri Kund is the legendary place where Goddess Parvati did austerities for many years to be able to marry Lord Shiva. It is 334 kilometres from Gangotri. Gauri Kund is the last bus stop on the way to Kedarnath. There is a hot sulphur water spring here marking the place where Parvati did the penance. Next to the spring is **Gauri Devi Temple** dedicated to Parvati.

Sirkata Ganesha Temple

There is a temple of *sirkata* Ganesha (the beheaded Ganesha) about a half kilometre from Gauri Kund. The *Skanda Purana* says this was the place where Lord Shiva beheaded his son Ganesha and then gave him an elephant's head.

▲ **The holy bells of Kedarnath**

BADRINATH
(Panch Prayag)

Against the backdrop of the Neelkanth Peak, nestled between the Nara and Narayana mountains by the banks of the River Alakananda lies the fourth Himalayan Dhaam — Badrinath.

We have already discussed about Badrinath Dhaam earlier in **Chaar Dhaam** *chapter on page 12.*

Here we shall discuss only **Panch Prayag**, *the five confluences located on the route between Rishikesh and Badrinath. Many pilgrims bathe at all five confluences before having darshan at Badrinath.*

Panch Prayag

There are seven holy rivers in the Himalayas called **Sapta Samudrik Teertha** — the Alakananda, Dhauli Ganga, Nandakini, Bhagirathi, Pindar Ganga, Mandakini and Nayar. They all are said to have come down on Lord Shiva's head together, but eventually fell to different places. There are five confluences (*prayag*) of the river Ganga on the way to Badrinath.

1. Dev Prayag

It is the confluence of the Bhagirathi and Alakananda. It is 90 kilometres from Rishikesh. At this point, the river takes the name Ganga. It is the second most important confluence in India next to Prayag of Allahabad, where the Yamuna, Ganga and Saraswati meet.

◀ **Rudranath Temple**

▲ **Dev Prayag**

It is believed that Lord Rama and Lakshmana performed a *yajna* (sacrifice) here to atone for killing Ravana, who was a Brahmin. There is an ancient **Raghunath Temple** here with a 15-foot-tall statue of Sri Rama. It was installed about 1250 years ago and is one of the 108 most important temples *(Divya Desams)* in India. In front of the temple is Garuda and to the left is Annapurna. Behind the temple and slightly uphill is Vamana's cave. Nearby is Lord Rama's stone throne.

2. Rudra Prayag

It is 70 kilometres north of Dev Prayag and this is where Mandakini from Kedarnath

◄ **Rudra Prayag**

meets Alakananda. There is a temple of Rudranath here. Nearby is a place where Narada Muni performed *tapasya*.

3. Karna Prayag

It is where the Alakananda meets the Pindar Ganga coming from the Pindar Glacier. Karna, the half-brother of the Pandavas, is said to have performed austerities here to please Lord Surya. Karna Prayag is 34 kilometres from Rudra Prayag.

4. Nanda Prayag

It is a small confluence of the Nandakini and Alakananda. Ravana underwent a penance and Nanda Maharaja performed a great sacrifice at this spot. Dushyant also married Shakuntala here and Kanva Rishi had his ashram at this place. There is a Gopalji Temple here.

5. Vishnu Prayag

It is where the Dhauli Ganga from Niti Valley meets the Alakananda from Badrinath. One road here via the Niti Pass, leads to Mount Kailash in Tibet which is considered to be Lord Shiva's abode.

SAPT PURI

ayodhya mathura maya kashi kanchi avantika
puri dwarawati chaiv saptaita mokshdayika

There are seven holy cities which bring salvation (*moksha*) to us.
These seven holy cities *(puri)* are:

1. Ayodhya – The Land of Lord Rama

2. Mathura – The Land of Lord Krishna

3. Haridwar – The Gateway to Lord Vishnu (Hari)

4. Varanasi – The City of Lord Shiva

5. Kanchipuram – The Golden City of Temples

6. Ujjain – The Holy Mokshapuri

7. Dwarka – The Capital of Lord Krishna (we have already discussed it in *Chaar Dhaam* section on page 20)

These seven cities are located in different corners of India, hence they act as strong links connecting India into one single nation.

Every Indian likes to visit these seven holy cities irrespective of caste, religion or state differences.

AYODHYA

Ayodhya is located on the banks of river Saryu in the State of Uttar Pradesh. Lord Rama was born in this holy city, which is about 150 kilometres east of Lucknow and 200 kilometres north-west of Varanasi.

Rama Janmabhoomi

This is where Lord Rama was said to have taken birth. There is a Lord Rama Temple here. At this location, there used to be the Babri Mosque, which was constructed in the 15th century by the Mughals. The mosque was destroyed in 1992.

Guptar Ghat

It is believed that Lord Rama left for heavenly abode at this place. Chakra Harji Vishnu, Gupta Harji and Raja Mandir are some of the famous temples here. There are many deities in the Chakra Harji Vishnu Temple, including what appears to be a very old carved Vishnu deity. There is also an imprint of Sri Rama's feet here. Guptar Ghat is located at a distance of about 20 minutes by a rickshaw from the bus depot in Faizabad.

Janma Sthana is where Lord Rama was said to have been brought up. There are over a hundred temples in Ayodhya.

Kanak Bhavan is also an interesting temple. It used to be the main temple of Ayodhya which was constructed by the King of Orchha. It is a huge temple. It was also called Sita Mahal. The main deities in this temple are Rama and Sita.

There is a popular temple dedicated to Hanuman called **Hanuman Garhi**. It is located on top of a hill. There are 60 steps which lead to the temple. A statue of Hauman in sitting posture is present in this temple. Another 6-inch-long statue of Hanuman is also here which is always covered with flowers.

◀ Ayodhya Temple

Then there is **Lakshman Ghat**, where Lakshman, the brother of Rama, had a bath. Rama is also said to have performed a *yajna* at **Treta Kay Mandir**. Kaushalya, the mother of Rama, is said to have established the **Kshireshwara Nath Temple** for Sita.

Bharat Kund, at Nandigram, 20 kilometres from Ayodhya, is said to be the place where Bharat ruled while Rama was in exile for 14 years.

A little north of Rama Janmabhoomi is *Swarga Dwar* or **Rama Ghat**, which is an important bathing ghat.

▲ Lord Rama, Lakshman, Sita and Hanuman

Dashrath Teertha is 12 kilometres away from Rama Ghat. It is believed that the last rites of King Dashrath, father of Lord Rama, were performed here.

Brahma Kund was built by Lord Brahma when he first visited Ayodhya.

Sita Kund is also a prominent place. It is said that a dip in this kund is enough to absolve us of all our sins.

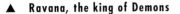

▲ **Ravana, the king of Demons**

Nageshwarnath Temple is the temple established by Kush, the elder son of Rama. According to the legend Kush lost his armlet, while bathing in the river Saryu. The armlet was picked up by a *nag-kanya*, who fell in love with him. As she was a devotee of Shiva, Kush erected this temple for her. This is believed to be the only temple to have survived till the time of Vikramaditya. With the help of this very temple, Vikramaditya was able to locate Ayodhya and the sites of various shrines here. Shivratri is celebrated with great pomp and grandeur here.

Tulsichaura is the place where Tulsidas composed *Ramacharitmanas*, the Hindi version of Ramayana.

Tulsi Smarak Bhawan was built in memory of the poet Goswami Tulsidas. This monument is used for religious sermons, prayer meetings, discussions, and the singing of devotional songs. It houses the **Ayodhya Shodh Sansthan**, which treasures a large collection of literary works of Swami Tulsidas. A cultural centre of performing arts also functions here.

Ramkatha Museum, a museum constructed in Ayodhya in 1988, collects and preserves the antiquities related to the life of Lord Rama.

MATHURA

Mathura and Vrindavan are the most important Vaishnava holy places in India. This is because Mathura is the birthplace of Lord Krishna and Vrindavan is where he spent his childhood.

Krishna Janmasthan

The main temple here is called the **Keshava Deo Temple**. The deity of Lord Keshava or Krishna was installed here by Vajranabha. The central deities in the temple are Radha-Krishna. On the left altar, by the entrance door, are Lord Jagannath, Balarama and Subhadra, being looked at by Shri Chaitanya. On the right altar are Sita, Rama and Lakshman. Across from them is Hanuman. There is a Shivalingam called Sri Keshavaeshwar in front of the deities of Sita and Rama. Directly across this Shivalingam is the statue of Goddess Durga.

There have been several major temples built on this site. The first temple here was constructed almost 5000 years ago by Vajranabha, the great grandson of Lord Krishna. The next big temple was constructed here during the time of the great Emperor Chandragupta Vikamaditya in around 400 AD. This temple was so grand that it was said that neither painting nor description could do justice to it. This temple was destroyed by Mahmud of Ghazni. During the reign of Jahangir, Raja Veer Singh Deva Bundela of Orchha constructed another temple about 250 feet high. In 1669, Aurangzeb destroyed this temple and constructed a mosque, which is still there, built from the materials of the temple.

Construction started on the present temple in 1951 and the deities were installed in 1958. Next to the temple is a small temple that looks like a prison cell, where Lord Krishna was born. At this small temple, there are deities of Vasudeva, Devaki, and four-armed Krishna.

Vishrama Ghat is a bathing ghat on the bank of the Yamuna River where Krishna rested after killing

▲ Vishrama Ghat, Mathura

King Kansa. It is said that Lord Varaha also rested here after killing Hiranyakashipu. There are 5000-year-old idols of Yamuna Devi and her brother Yamaraj here. Every day there is a sunset *arati* offered to the Yamuna River.

Ranga Bhoomi is located just opposite the Main Post Office in Mathura. Krishna killed Kansa here on the hill called **Kansa Teela**.

Behind this hill is the place where Krishna crowned Ugrasen as the king of Mathura. Nearby is the **Rangeshwara Mahadev Temple** which houses the Shivalingam which is worshipped by wrestlers before their wrestling match.

Other Places

Many incidences from the *Srimad Bhagavatam* and other *Puranas* took place in Mathura. King Ambarish waited at **Ambarish Teela** in Mathura for Sage Durvasa to return from being chased by Lord Vishnu's *chakra*.

At **Bali Teela**, King Bali performed his great *yajna* to take over the Universe and Lord Vamana begged three steps of land from him at this place.

The **Dwarkadhish Temple** was built in 1814. It is a popular temple in the heart of the town.

▲ **Lord Krishna and Radha**

Vrindavan

Mathura is incomplete without the mention of Vrindavan. It is here in Vrindavan that Lord Krishna spent his childhood days. Vrindavan is 12 kilometres from Mathura. It has a small town atmosphere with narrow streets and not much traffic on the roads. There are over 5000 temples here.

▼ **Entering the Krishna Janmabhoomi Temple**

Krishna Balarama Temple

This temple has deities of Gaura-Nitai (left altar), Krishna-Balarama (middle altar) and Radha-Shyama Sundara (right altar). In front of the temple is the *Samadhi Mandir* of Bhaktivedanta Swami Prabhupada, the founder of the International Society for Krishna Consciousness (ISKCON).

Govindji Temple

Govindji Temple was built in 1590 by King Mansingh of Jaipur, and was originally seven storeys high, with an altar of marble, silver and gold. The original deity of Govindji was removed from this temple when the Mughal Emperor Aurangzeb tried to destroy it. It is now installed in a temple right outside the King of Jaipur's palace.

Madan Mohan Temple

This 60-foot-high temple was built in 1580 on a 50-foot-high hill called Aditya Teela, next to the Yamuna River. The original Madan Mohan deity was moved from Vrindavan to Jaipur when the Mughal Emperor Aurangzeb attacked Vrindavan in 1670.

◀ Madan Mohan Temple, Vrindavan

Radha Damodara Temple

This temple was founded by Jiva Goswami. The main deities here are Radha-Damodara. There is a *Govardhana Shila* in this temple that has Lord Krishna's footprint on it.

Radha Gopinath Temple

On the altar are deities of Radha and her sister Ananga Manjari. Gopinathji was installed by Vajranabha, the great grandson of Krishna.

Radha Raman Temple

Gopal Bhatta Goswami established this temple. The deity of Radha-Raman was manifested from one of Gopal Bhatta Goswami's *shaligram shilas* on the full moon day of *Vaishakha* (April/May) in 1542. This event is celebrated every year by bathing the deity with 100 litres of milk and other auspicious items.

Banke Bihari Temple

This temple was established by Haridas Swami. He discovered the Banke Bihari deity at Nidhivan. Banke Bihari was moved here when this temple was constructed in 1864. This is the most popular temple in Vrindavan. The curtain before the deities is not left open like at other temples.

Every few minutes, the curtain is drawn and then pulled again. Only one day in the year, i.e. on *Akshaya Tritiya*, the lotus feet of the deity can be seen.

Gopishwara Mahadev Temple

The Shivalingam in this temple was installed by Vajranabha, the great grandson of Krishna. It is said that the big peepal tree here is the *Kalpavriksha* (wish-fulfilling tree).

Kesi Ghat is on the bank of the Yamuna River. Lord Krishna killed the Kesi demon here. There is a Yamuna *arati* performed here every day at sunset. Krishna rested at **Chir Ghat** after killing the Kesi demon.

Rangaji Temple

Built in 1851, this temple is dedicated to Lord Ranganatha depicted as Lord Vishnu in his *sheshashayi* pose, reclining on the coils of sheshanag. The temple follows the Dravidian style of architecture and has a high *gopuram* of six storeys and a gold-plated *dhwaja stambha*, which is 50 feet high. A water tank and a scenic garden are located within the temple enclosure. The annual festival of Jal Vihar of the presiding deity is celebrated with great show and splendour at the tank. The temple is also popular for its Brahmotsav celebration in March/April, commonly known as the *Rath ka mela*. The ten-day-long festivities are marked by the pulling of the *rath* by the devotees from the temple to the adjacent gardens.

Seva Kunja

At this place, Krishna is still believed to massage Radha's feet and adorn her hair with flowers. Once Krishna pushed his flute into the ground

▲ Kusuma Sarovar, Vrindavan

here and created a small kund, called Lalita Kund, to quench the thirst of Lalita, a *gopika*. No one is allowed within the enclosure at night. The numerous monkeys that are there during the day also leave at night.

Vrindavan Parikrama

It is customary for devotees to walk around the town of Vrindavan. There is a *parikrama* path that goes around the town. This path is one street over from the ISKCON temple. It takes two or three hours to go around the town.

Braja Mandala Parikrama

Braja Mandal Parikrama is organised by ISKCON every year in October/ November. This one-month walking tour takes one through all the twelve forests in Vrindavan. The *parikarma* visits most

▲ Ancient yaksha sculpture

of the major places in the Braja area, including Mathura, Radha Kund, Varsana, Nandagrama, Gokula, Vrindavan, and Govardhana Hill. Devotees generally walk barefoot here, though shoes are allowed.

▲ The Sacred Shivalingam

HARIDWAR

*Haridwar is on the western bank of the river Ganga, at the foot of the Himalayan Mountains. Haridwar means the gateway to Hari (Lord Vishnu). It is also called **Gangadwar** because this is the place where the holy Ganga enters the plains. Nearby, at **Sapt Sarovar**, the Ganga splits into seven streams to please the seven Rishis performing austerities there. The main natural rivulet of the Ganga, called **Neel Dhara**, flows to the east of the city.*

Kumbh Mela

Haridwar is one of the four places where Kumbh Mela is held every 12 years. The other three places are Allahabad (Prayag), Nasik and Ujjain.

▼ Haridwar, the gateway to Lord Vishnu

One of the main bathing days is the first day of *Vaishakha* (April/May) when the Hindu solar year begins. Every year thousands of people come to Haridwar to bathe in the Ganga on this day.

Har-ki-Pauri Ghat

The name *Har-ki-Pauri* means the feet of Hari (Lord Vishnu). The footprints of Lord Vishnu are imprinted on the wall of the temple dedicated to Vishnu.

▲ **The consecrated shores of Haridwar**

This ghat is supposed to be the exact spot where the Ganga enters the plains after leaving the mountains. There is a temple in reverence to the Goddess Ganga. Every evening, an *arati* is performed in the honour of the sacred River Ganga. The *arati* consists of offering earthen lamps to the river amidst chanting and ringing of bells. The ashes of the dead are also cast into the Ganga River at the southern part of the ghat.

Mansa Devi Temple

This temple is situated on Bilwa Parbat, a hill above the city. Mansa Devi is a form of *Shakti*. From top of the hill, you get a bird's eye view of Haridwar, the Ganga valley and the Himalayan peaks.

▲ **Ganga arati**

Other Places

Bhimgoda Kund is said to have been created by Bhima, one of the Pandavas, with a blow of his knee. It is about half-a-kilometre upstream from Har-ki-Pauri ghat, just off the road on the way to Sapta Rishi Ashram.

▲ **Har-ki-Pauri Ghat**

Kushavarta Ghat, about half-a-kilometre south of Har-ki-Pauri Kund, is the place where Dattatreya is believed to have performed penance by standing on one foot for a thousand years.

Gau Ghat is between Har-ki-Pauri and Kushavarta Ghat. It is said one can be salvaged from the sin of killing and eating a cow by bathing here. Lord Vishnu is said to have bathed at Vishnu Ghat.

Sapta Rishi Ashram, about 6 kilometres from Haridwar on the banks of the Ganga, is where the river is said to have divided to avoid displeasing the seven *Rishis* meditating there.

About 4 kilometres from Haridwar on the eastern summits of the Shivalik Hills are the **Chandi Devi** and **Anjani Devi** temples. At the foot of the hills are the **Gauri-Shankar** and **Neeleshwar** temples.

Gauri Kund is a holy well about 4 feet wide, which is one of the four main bathing places in Haridwar. The other three include Har-ki-Pauri, Neel Dhara and Kankhal, by the Daksha Mahadeva Temple.

In Haridwar, there are three old temples called **Narayana-shila**, **Maya Devi**, and **Bhairava Temple**. Maya Devi is a three-headed, four-armed deity, who is shown killing a prostrated figure.

▲   **The pious river Ganga**

Kankhal

Kankhal was the ancient capital of Prajapati Daksha. It is about 4 kilometres south of Haridwar. Daksha, the son of Lord Brahma and father of Sati, once performed a *yajna* at this place, where he invited everyone except his son-in-law Lord Shiva. Sati went to attend the *yajna* but her father did not even talk to her and bad-mouthed about her husband, Lord Shiva. Feeling greatly insulted, Sati burned herself in the blazing fire of the *yajna*. Hearing about his wife's death, Lord Shiva then created Virabhadra, a fearful black demon, who had thousands of arms equipped with various weapons. Lord Shiva sent Virabhadra and his followers to ruin the sacrifice and cut off Daksha's head. On fulfilling his job, Virabhadra threw Daksha's head in the sacrificial fire. Later, at the request of Lord Brahma, Shiva restored Daksha to life; but since his head was destroyed in the fire, he was given a goat's head.

The **Daksheshwara Mahadev Shiva Temple** is also known as Daksha Prajapati Temple. It is said to have been built in commemoration of Lord Shiva. Next to this temple on the bank of the Ganga is Daksha Ghat.

Sati Kund, on Kankhal Jwalapur Road, marks the spot where Sati burned herself.

Rishikesh

Rishikesh is located 24 kilometres from Haridwar. Ganga leaves the Himalayan Mountains from Rishikesh. This place is famous as a Yoga and meditation Centre. There are many ashrams here.

▼   **A panoramic view**

▲ **Pujas in Haridwar**

The town got its name when Lord Hrishikesh, another name for Lord Vishnu, came before Raibhya Rishi who was performing *tapasya* (penance) here and granted him *darshan*.

Rishikesh is the place where most pilgrims begin their pilgrimage of Himalayan *Chaar Dhaam* that include Yamunotri, Gangotri, Kedarnath and Badrinath.

Rishikesh is at the meeting point of the Ganga and Chandrabhaga Rivers. Most of the religious spots are along the banks of these rivers.

Bharat Temple

Despite the name, the presiding deity at this temple is Lord Narayana and not Bharat. It is a very old temple with a high wall around it. It is located in the heart of Rishikesh. There is an inscription on the temple that says that the temple was renovated by Adi Shankaracharya.

Lakshman Jhoola

Lakshman Jhoola is about 3 kilometres north of Rishikesh. At this place Lakshman, Rama's younger brother, is said to have performed penance. There is a Lakshman Temple here by the bridge.

Triveni Ghat is the main bathing ghat where the Ganga, Yamuna and Saraswati Rivers flow together. *Pinda shraddha* or offering to the forefathers is performed here.

Shatrughana Temple is about 4.5 kilometres from Rishikesh. It is dedicated to Shatrughana, the youngest brother of Lord Rama.

At **Muni-ki-Reti**, the Ganga emerges out of the Himalayan foothills.

The **Balaji** and **Chandramouleshwara** Temples are constructed in the Dravidian style. They are run by the same board that runs the temple in Tirupati and the temple rituals are also the same as those at Tirupati.

Neelkantha Mahadev Temple is situated at a height of 5,500 feet above sea level and is about 11 kilometres from Lakshman Jhoola.

VARANASI

▶ **An 11th century statue of Lord Shiva**

Varanasi or Kashi is considered the oldest inhabited city in the world. There are 23,000 temples in Varanasi. The city of Varanasi is on the western bank of the Ganga River. The old section of the city by the river is where the bathing ghats and temples are located.

*It is said that the first Jyotirlingam, the fiery pillar of light, came to the earth here and flared into the sky. Therefore Varanasi is also called Kashi, the City of Lights. The Ganga, which normally flows south-east, reverses its course and flows northwards for a while at Varanasi, which is considered very auspicious. There are 81 bathing ghats and other holy kunds in Varanasi. The three most important ghats are **Manikarnika, Dashashwamedha** and **Panchaganga**. **Asi Sangam** and **Varana Sangam** are also important ghats.*

Vishwanath Temple

The present temple, dedicated to Lord Shiva, was built by Rani Ahilyabai Holkar of Indore in 1776. It is also called the Golden Temple because of the gold plating on the *shikhars* (roof over the altar) by Maharaja Ranjit Singh in 1835.

The *lingam* is on a golden altar. As one enters the temple, to the left is the deity of Vishnu who is supposed to be worshipped along with Vishwanath. Right outside the Golden Temple is the shrine of Shanidev (Saturn) who is worshipped to get rid of misfortune.

A major temple, dedicated to **Annapurna**, is located in the same alley as the Vishwanath Temple. *Anna* means 'food' and *Purna* means 'someone who fills'.

Dhundhiraj Ganesha is a small, yet important Ganesha temple on Vishwanath Lane, about a five-minute-walk from the Vishwanath Temple. Sakshi Vinayaka is the Ganesha deity. *Sakshi* literally means 'the witness' and Vinayaka is another name of Ganesha.

Dashashwamedha Ghat

This is the main bathing ghat in the town. The area around this ghat is the main centre of activity in the city. It is said that Lord Brahma performed a *Dashashwamedha Yajna* (ten-horse-sacrifice) here.

Manikarnika Ghat

Manikarnika means 'jewelled earring'. It got this name when Lord Shiva's earring fell into the well. It is believed that this well was dug by Lord Vishnu with

◀ **Varanasi, the city blessed by Goddess Ganga**

▲ Holy ghats

▲ The hallowed city of Varanasi

his discus *(chakra)* and filled by water as his first act of creation. There is an image of Lord Vishnu in the northern wall of the kund. Lord Vishnu's footprints are located at **Chakrapushkarini**, which is between Manikarnika Kund and the river. Manikarnika Ghat is considered the holiest of all ghats. There is a major cremation ground right next to this ghat. Normally, the cremation ground is outside the town. Here the cremation ground is in the middle of the city because death in Kashi is considered a great blessing.

Bindu Madhava Temple

It is an important Vishnu temple. The present deity of Bindu Madhava is in a small temple. It is located just above the **Panchaganga Ghat**.

Adi Keshava Temple is located where the Varana River flows into the Ganga. Lord Vishnu is said to have first put his feet here when he came to Varanasi.

Durga Temple and **Sankat Mochan Temple** are both located in the southern part of the town.

▲ Lord Shiva in dancing mudra

▶ Durga Temple from outside

KANCHIPURAM

Kanchipuram is known as the 'Golden City of Temples'. It has over a hundred temples now, but at one time it is said to have had one thousand temples. Kanchipuram is believed to give eternal happiness to everyone who goes there. The myth says that Brahma **(Ka)** *worshipped* **(anchi)** *Lord Vishnu at this city* **(puram)** *and that is how the city got the name 'Kanchipuram'.*

Kanchipuram is located 71 kilometres south-west of Chennai on the Vegavati River. The city is divided into two main parts — **Shivakanchi**, *which is the northern suburb and* **Vishnukanchi**, *which is the extreme eastern section of town.*

Kailashanatha *and* **Vaikuntha Perumal** *temples were built by the Pallavas.* **Varadaraja**, **Kamakshi** *and* **Ekambareshwara** *temples were originally built by the Cholas, but were added onto by the Vijayanagar and Nayaka rulers.*

Kanchipuram is famous for its hand-woven silk fabrics and saris. The weavers use the highest quality silk and pure gold thread.

Divya Desam Temples

There are thirteen *Divya Desam* temples in the area of Kanchipuram. They are — Sri Vaikuntha Perumal Temple, Sri Varadaraja Temple, Sri Adi Varaha Perumal Temple, Sri Pandava Dootha Perumal Temple, Sri Deepa Prakasha Temple, Sri Yathoktakari Temple, Sri Alagiyasingar Temple, Sri Nilathingal Thundathan Perumal Temple in the Ekambareshwara Temple, Sri Ashtabhujam Perumal Temple, Sri Pavalavannar Temple, Sri Ulagalanda Perumal Temple and Sri Vijaya Raghava Perumal Temple. The Sri Ulagalanda Perumal Temple has four *Divya Desam* temples in it —Peragathan and Ooragam (always mentioned together), Neeragham, Karagham and Karvannam.

Sri Varadaraja Temple

This is a major Vishnu temple built by the Vijayanagar kings in the 12th century. *Varada* means the one who bestows benedictions and *raja* means king. Thus, Varadaraja means the king of those who give benedictions. It is said that Brahma made a fire sacrifice to manifest Vishnu on an altar here. The present temple is said to reflect the same altar. The deity is also called Devaraja Swami and Arulalar, which means the source of all grace and the provider of all boons. The lord is also named Hastigirinatha.

◀ **The Ekambareshwara Temple**

Other names of the deity are Devaki Devarajan, Kari Varadan, Paranatartiharan, and Manicka Varadan. Lord Varadaraja is standing facing west and his four hands hold *shankha* (conch), *chakra* (disc), *gada* (club), and *padma* (lotus). His consort is Sri Perundevi Thayar (Lakshmi), who has her own temple to the right of the main temple.

This temple has a 90-foot-high *gopuram* and a 100-pillared *mandapa* with exquisite sculptures. Mainly *avatars* of Vishnu and scenes from the *Mahabharata* and *Ramayana* are carved on the pillars. Its main hall is supported by giant pillars, each carved from a different rock.

The temple is on top of **Hastigiri**, which is an elephant-shaped rock. This hill is so called because the *hasti* (elephant) *Gajendra*, worshipped the Lord on this *giri* (hill) in *Tretayuga*.

The temple is spread across 23 acres, which is one of the biggest areas covered by a temple in India. **Anata teertham**, the temple tank, is located to the north of the 100-pillared *mandapa* hall.

The temple chariot is 60 feet high and is a veritable temple on wheels. The temple has an exquisite collection of jewellery. One of the necklaces was given by General Clive, the British Governor of the Madras Presidency. It is said that Clive came on the day of the *Garuda seva* of Lord Varadaraja and he presented his wife's necklace to the priest to adorn the Lord. The necklace is known as **Clive Makarakandi** and is used to decorate Lord Varadaraja on the Garudotsavam day.

▲ **The holy shrine of Varadaraja**

The main festival here is the Brahmotsav festival celebrated in May-June, which is attended by thousands of people. During this festival, the deity is carried out in a procession.

▲ **Lord Vishnu**

Sri Vaikuntha Perumal Temple

This Lord Vishnu temple was built in the late 8th century. It has three sanctums, one above the other, where Lord Vishnu is standing, sitting and reclining respectively. The goddess' name is Sri Vaikunthavalli Thayar. This temple is thoroughly decorated with paintings on the walls. Its sculptures depict the wars fought between the Pallavas and the Chalukyas. The temple was built by Nandivaram Palavamalla.

Sri Ulagalanda Perumal Temple

This temple is dedicated to Vamana. The main deity is called Ulagalanda Perumal, the Lord who measured the world with his three steps. Trivikrama is another name for Lord Vamana, who begged from Bali the amount of land that he could cover in three steps. The consort of Ulagalanda Perumal is Amrithavalli Thayar.

This temple has four *Divya Desam* shrines in it — Peragathan and Ooragam, Neeragham, Karagham, and Karvannam shrines.

The shrine of Adi Shesha is called Ooragam. It means snake. Adi Shesha is the divine snake used as a couch by the Lord Vishnu.

Peragathan (Trivikrama) and **Ooragam** *(Adi Shesha)* are together referred to as one *Divya Desam* shrine.

Behind a beautiful 16-pillared *mandapa* in the second prakaram is the shrine of **Neeragathan**, who is also called Jagadeeshwara Perumal. It is said that the Lord gave *darshan* to sage Markandeya here.

In the third prakaram of the temple is the *Divya Desam* shrine of **Karunakara Perumal**. His consort is known as Padmamani Thayar.

The fourth *Divya Desam* shrine in the temple is **Karvannam**, who is also known as Navaneeta Chora. His consort is called Komalavalli Thayar.

Sri Vijaya Raghava Perumal Temple

This temple is 7 kilometres from Kanchipuram in the town of Thiruputkuli. The Lord here is known as Vijaya Raghava, which means 'Rama the winner'. The goddess of the temple is known as Maragathavalli Thayar. In front of the temple is a bathing tank called **Jatayupushkarini**. On a hill to the east of the tank is a temple dedicated to Jatayu, the gigantic vulture who was killed by Ravana.

Sri Ashtabhujam Perumal Temple

In this temple, the idol of Lord Vishnu has eight arms. *Ashta* means eight and *bhuja* means arms. It is said that when goddess Saraswati sent an army of demons to ruin the sacrifice performed by Brahma, they were all killed by Lord Vishnu. She then sent Sarabha, a beast with eight legs. To defeat this beast, Lord Vishnu assumed this form with eight arms equipped with eight weapons. The goddess is known as Puspakavalli Thayar. There is also a deity of Varahadeva, Lord Vishnu in his boar incarnation, in this temple.

Pandava Dootha Perumal Temple

The Pandava Dootha Perumal Temple is located near Ekambareshwara temple. The main Vishnu deity is in a sitting posture. It signifies the *Vishwarupa* (universal) form of the Lord.

▲ Sri Varadaraja Temple

Sri Deepa Prakasha Temple

In this temple, the presiding deity of Lord Vishnu is named Sri Deepa Prakasha which means the

▲ Sri Vaikuntha Perumal Temple

'light of the lamp'. His consorts are Sri Devi and Bhu Devi. The temple is also known as Vilokkoli Koyil.

Lord Vishnu is known as Deepa Prakasha here because he intercepted and made a lamp out of the fire that goddess Saraswati started in order to burn the sacrificial site where Lord Brahma was performing the *Aswamedha Yajna*.

Sri Yathoktakari Temple

In this temple, Lord Vishnu is in a lying posture. The main deity is known as Lord Yathoktakari because he accepted the request of Tirumalisai Alwar, his devotee, to get up and follow him out of Kanchipuram and to again return and lie down. *Yathokta* means 'as requested' and *kari* means 'the person who did it'. The consort of Lord Yathoktakari is known as Komalavalli.

Sri Alagiyasingar Temple

Lord Vishnu is known here as Mukunda Nayaka. It is said that Lord Vishnu took the form of

Narasimha and fought with the demon Kapalika to save Brahma's *yajna*. This temple is less than a kilometre from the Deepa Prakasha Temple.

Sri Pavalavannar Temple

The presiding deity of Lord Vishnu here is in a sitting posture on the divine couch of the Adi Shesha. This *Divya Desam* temple is near the Kamakshi Amman Temple. The consort of Pavalavannar is Pavalavalli Thayar.

Sri Adi Varaha Perumal Temple

It is one of the Divya Desam temples. It is located within the temple walls. This shrine is located to the left of the entrance to the altar of Kamakshi Amman.

In the west side of the temple lies Pancha Ganga Tank. It is believed to contain water from five faces of Shiva. There is a shrine having three floors, each having a Vishnu deity in different postures — standing, sitting and reclining.

Other Temples

Sri Ekambareshwara Temple

This temple, dedicated to Lord Shiva, is the largest temple in Kanchipuram. It is also known as the Ekambaranatha Temple. It has a towering 188-foot-high *gopuram* (gateway) built by Krishna Deva Raya of the Vijayanagar empire in 1509. No two towers of the temple are opposite each other nor are the walls of the temple parallel to each other. There are almost no right angles in the temple. It has a 1000-pillared hall with intricately and beautifully carved pillars.

There is a mango tree behind the main temple that is considered to be 3,500 years old.

▲ Devotees outside the temple

It has four branches which represent the four Vedas. Each leaf of this tree is of a different shape. The fruit from each branch has a different taste. In the path around the tree is a Shivalingam made of 108 small *lingams* and another one made up of 1008 *lingams*. The huge lingam is known as the *Prithvi-lingam* (Earth) one of the five element *lingams*. The other four are the *Agni-lingam* (fire) at Thiruvannamali, the *Appu-lingam* (water) at Jambukeswara, the *Vayu-lingam* (air) at Kalahasti, and the *Akasha-lingam* (ether) at Chidambaram.

▲ Varadaraja Perumal Temple

There is a Vishnu temple within the temple complex, which is one of the *Divya Desam* shrines. The deity is named Nilathingal Thundatthan Vishnu.

Kailashanatha Temple

This sandstone temple, dedicated to Lord Shiva, was built by Rajasimha Pallava in the 7th century. It is one of the earliest examples of Dravidian architecture and is one of the most beautiful temples in Kanchipuram.

Kailashanatha means Lord of Mount Kailash. It is famous for its sculptures. Most famous of these is the sculpture of Ardhanareshwara, who has a veena in one hand. There are paintings on the inner walls of the shrine. The outer wall of the temple has 58 small shrines showing different aspects of Shiva.

Kamakshi Amman Temple

This temple is dedicated to goddess Kamakshi (Parvati), the love-eyed goddess. *Kamakshi* means 'the one who has eyes full of love'.

Right in front of Sri Kamakshi is the **Sri Chakra**. All worships and sacrifices are offered to the Sri Chakra.

UJJAIN

▶ **Vigrahalingam**

Maharaja Jai Singh built an observatory in Ujjain (Madhya Pradesh) as he did in Jaipur (Rajasthan) and Delhi. According to the Indian astrology, the first meridian of longitude passes through Ujjain. The modern calculations prove that the Tropic of Cancer passes through the centre of town. It was in Ujjain that Bhaktisiddhanta Saraswati Maharaja Bimal Prasad wrote **Surya Siddhanta***, a great astronomical treatise that won him the title* **'Siddhanta Saraswati'***.*

Mahakala of Ujjain is known among the twelve celebrated Jyotirlingams in India. The glory of **Mahakaleshwar Temple** *of Ujjain has been vividly described in various Puranas. Starting with Kalidasa, many Sanskrit poets have eulogised this temple in emotive terms. Ujjain used to be central point of the calculation of the Indian time and Shiva, in all his splendour as Mahakala was considered as the presiding deity of Ujjain.*

Ujjain is another site for Kumbh Mela held once every 12 years. River Shipra flows by Ujjain. It is considered as sacred as the Ganga. Kumbh Mela is held at the banks of the river Shipra.

Vikram Kirti Temple

This temple houses the Scindia Oriental Research Institute, an archaeological museum and art gallery. The Institute has a rare collection of 18,000 old manuscripts including palm leaf and bark *(bhoja patra)* manuscripts. There is an illustrated *Srimad Bhagavatam* manuscript in which actual gold and silver have been employed for the paintings.

Harsiddhi Temple

The Harsiddhi Temple is where the idol of Annapurna resides between Mahalaksmi and Mahasaraswati. According to the *Shiva Purana*, this is where the elbow of Sati dropped, after she burned herself in the sacrificial fire. The idol of Annapurna is painted in a dark vermillion colour. There is an enormous banyan tree *'Siddhavat'* on the bank of the Shipra River.

It is believed to be comparable to *Akshayavat* (eternal banyan tree) in Prayag and Gaya. It is believed that Parvati performed penance at Siddhavat.

◀ **Mahakaleshwar Temple**

Mangalnath Temple

According to the *Matsya Purana*, Mangalnath is the birthplace of *Mangal* (Mars). In ancient times, it was famous for a clear view of the red planet Mars and hence suitable for astronomical studies.

Navgraha Temple

This temple is dedicated to the nine planets. It is situated at Triveni Ghat on the Shipra River. It attracts large crowds on new moon days falling on Saturdays.

Bade Ganeshji ka Mandir

Near the Mahakaleshwar Temple tank is the Bade Ganeshji ka Mandir with a very large deity of Ganesha called Chintaman Ganesha, with his consorts Riddhi and Siddhi. The temple also houses a *pancha-mukhi* (five-faced) Hanuman and the *Navgrahas* (nine planetary deities).

Rama Mandir and Rama Mandir Ghat

The clean, quiet and scenic Rama Mandir and its ghat is the ideal place to spend some quiet moments by the banks of Shipra River.

Kal Bhairav Temple

This temple is mentioned in the *Skanda Purana*. The Kapalika and Aghotra sects venerate Kal Bhairav and Ujjain was a prominent centre for both the sects. Even today, the ritual offering to the deity is the liquor. Kal Bhairav Temple is surrounded by a small, clean and well kept garden.

There is a deep and narrow cave in the courtyard which houses a temple of Patal Bhairav. A little further down

▲ **The illustrious Kumbh Mela**

the road, there is Vikrant Bhairav Shrine. Both these places are a must-visit for the tantriks.

Bhartrihari Caves

Bhartrihari was a great scholar and poet. He was the step-brother of King Vikramaditya. He renounced worldly life to escape complicated matters of the heart. He had discovered that his favourite queen loved someone who was himself in love with a beautiful courtesan, while that courtesan could think of no one but Bhartrihari. Having renounced the world, Bhartrihari lived and meditated in these caves.

▲ Outside the Mahakaleshwar Temple

▼ **A sadhu**

DWADASH JYOTIRLINGAM

Since times immemorial, India has been home to different sects who follow different faiths and live together in peace and harmony. The followers of Shaivism (devotees of Lord Shiva) worship at the twelve Jyotirlingams which have been installed at different places all over India.

It has been mentioned in Shiva Purana that Lord Shiva resides in twelve teerthas known as twelve Jyotirlingams. As and when his devotees prayed to him, he appeared then and there and stayed on as Jyotirlingam. It is believed that Lord Shiva himself blesses his devotees in these places.

The twelve Jyotirlingams of Lord Shiva are at these places:

1. **Somnath in Saurashtra** *(Gujarat)*
2. **Mallikarjuna in Srisailam** *(Andhra Pradesh)*
3. **Mahakaleshwar in Ujjain** *(Madhya Pradesh)*
4. **Omkareshwar in Shivpuri** *(Madhya Pradesh)*
5. **Kashi Vishwanath in Varanasi** *(Uttar Pradesh)*
6. **Baidyanath in Deoghar** *(Jharkhand)*
7. **Kedareshwar in Kedarnath** *(Uttarakhand)*
8. **Nageshwar in Dwarka** *(Gujarat)*
9. **Ghrishneshwar in Aurangabad** *(Maharashtra)*
10. **Triambakeshwar in Nasik** *(Maharashtra)*
11. **Rameshwar in Rameshwaram** *(Tamil Nadu)*
12. **Bhimshankar in Manchar** *(Maharashtra)*

SOMNATH

▲ **Shivalingam**

Somnath is on the extreme south-western coast of Gujarat on the Arabian Sea. Somnath is famous as the place where Lord Krishna was shot in the foot by a hunter.

One of the 12 Jyotirlingams is at the Somnath Temple.

Somnath Jyotirlingam Temple

This temple, housing one of the 12 Shiva Jyotirlingams, is on the shore of the Arabian Sea. It is said that this temple was originally built by Soma, the Moon God, to atone for the curse Daksha had put on him. Soma was cursed by Daksha for being partial towards Rohini over his other wives, who were the daughters of Daksha. Because of the curse, the moon began to wane. Daksha then advised him to go to *Prabhasa* to get rid of the curse and regain his light. Soma did that and the place came to be known as **Prabhasa Patan**.

Somnath means the 'Lord of the Moon'. Somnath is located where the River Saraswati flows into the sea. This temple is said to have been built by the Moon with gold, then rebuilt by Ravana with silver, then rebuilt by Krishna with wood, and later by Bhima from stone. The temple was raided and destroyed by Mahmud of Ghazni in 1026.

A long history is associated with the Somnath Temple. The first temple of Somnath is believed to have existed in the pre-Christian era. The Maitraka Kings of Vallabhi in Gujarat built the second temple. The third temple was built by the Pratihara King Nagabhata II. The fourth temple was built by the Paramara King Bhoj of Malwa, whereas the Solanki King Kumarpal built the fifth temple. This temple was again destroyed by Mughal emperor Aurangzeb. The present temple is the seventh temple and has been rebuilt and taken care by Shri Somnath trust. The present temple rebuilt in 1950 stands at the exact place where the original temple was situated. You can see the remains of an ancient temple right next to the present temple.

◄ **Somnath Temple**

MALLIKARJUNA

This temple, dedicated to Lord Shiva, is nestled in the Reshabagiri Hills on the southern bank of the Krishna River. It is to the west of Vijayawada. It is also known as Sriparvata.

Mallikarjuna Swami Temple

The Mallikarjuna Swami Temple is one of the 12 Jyotirlingam Shiva temples in the country. The main temple has four lofty towers and was built by King Harihara Raya in 1404. The temple is surrounded by 8.5-metre-high wall. As you enter this temple, you will first notice a well-carved *Mukha Mandapa* (hall) with a huge carved stone Nandi bull. The Lord's consort here is known as Bhramarambika.

To the right of the main temple is the **Vriddha Mallikarjuna Shivalingam** belonging to 7th century which is the original Shivalingam that was installed in this temple.

▲ Sculptures inside Mallikarjuna Swami Temple

It is believed that because this *lingam* was originally worshipped with jasmine or *mallika* flowers, it was given the name Mallikarjuna.

The myths suggest that this temple was visited by Lord Rama after he returned from Lanka. Lord Rama is said to have personally installed the **Sahasralingam** here. This Sahasralingam is surrounded by a three-headed Naga and consists of 1001 miniature *lingams*.

Behind the main temple and up a flight of stairs is the temple of the goddess Bhramarambika (Parvati) who is considered to have assumed the form of a bee to kill the demon Mahishasura. If you press your ear to a tiny hole on the exterior back wall of the sanctum, you can hear the buzzing of a bee.

The outer enclosure walls of the Mallikarjuna Temple have five regular rows of sculptures on the eastern, southern and northern walls.

▲ Mallikarjuna Swami Temple

MAHAKALESHWAR

Mahakaleshwar is in Ujjain in Madhya Pradesh. In Ujjain, this temple is located near a lake.

▲ **Shivalingam**

Mahakaleshwar Jyotirlingam Temple

This temple has five levels, one of which is underground. The temple itself is located in a spacious courtyard surrounded by massive walls. The *shikhar* (top) is adorned with sculptural finery. Brass lamps light the way to the underground sanctum.

Out of the 12 Jyotirlingams in India, the *lingam* at the Mahakal is believed to be *swayambhu* (born of itself), deriving *Shakti* (power) from within itself as against the other images and lingams which are ritually established and invested with *mantra-shakti*.

The idol of Mahakaleshwar is known to be Dakshinamurti, facing the south. This is a unique feature, upheld by *tantrik* tradition to be found only in Mahakaleshwar. It is not found in any of the other 11 Jyotirlingams. The idol of Lord Shiva is consecrated in the sanctum above the Mahakal shrine. The images of Ganesha, Parvati and Kartikeya are installed in the west, north and east of the sanctum sanctorum respectively. To the south is the image of Nandi.

The idol of Nagchandreshwar on the third storey is open for *darshan* only on the day of *Naga panchami*.

The central roof of the *garbha griha* is decked with the sacred *Rudrayantra* made of 100 kilograms of silver.

One of the rituals, the *Bhasma arati* involves smearing the *lingam* with still-hot ashes from the cremation grounds in homage to Shiva as the master of death. It is a ritual of symbolism. Death and life in Hindu tradition form parts of an inseparable continuum.

▲ **Mahakaleshwar Temple**

Legend has it that a demon named Dushana tormented the residents of Avanti and Shiva appeared from the ground and vanquished the demon, and then upon the request of the inhabitants of Avanti, took up permanent abode here as Mahakaleshwar Jyotirlingam. In Ujjain, there is a Parvati-Harasiddhi Devi Temple as well.

▲ The entrance to
Mahakaleshwar Jyotirlingam Temple

OMKARESHWAR

Omkareshwar is on Mandhata Island, which is 2 kilometres long and 1 kilometre wide, at the confluence of the Narmada and Kaveri rivers. All the temples on the island are dedicated to Lord Shiva. On the north side of the Narmada are a few old ruined temples dedicated to Lord Vishnu.

Omkareshwar Mandhata Temple

One of the 12 Jyotirlingams is located in Omkareshwar Mandhata Temple. The sculptures in this important Shiva temple are extremely detailed.

Besides Jyotirlingam, the island of Omkareshwar is in itself a sacred site. The island is naturally shaped so as to resemble the sacred *Om* symbol.

There is a traditional *parikrama* of the island that begins at the ghats below the temple and goes clockwise around the island. It is an 8-kilometre-walk and takes at least three hours. It is a comfortable walk until you reach the confluence of the Narmada and Kaveri rivers. From here, the path climbs along the north shore until you reach the Gauri Somnath Temple, which is surrounded by numerous sculptures. There is a huge Nandi carved of green stone in front of the **Gauri Somnath Temple**. There is a large Shivalingam in this temple. But the most inspiring of all sculptures, gateways and temples is the sacred meeting point of Narmada River with Kaveri River at the tip of the island where every stone is considered a Shivalingam.

After going up a gully you come to the **Surajkund Gate**, with 9-foot-high statues of

▲ **The revered Omkareshwar Ghats**

Arjuna and Bhima, the two Pandava brothers, on either side. Close to this place is the 10th century **Siddhnath Temple**, which is the oldest temple on the island and has elaborate carvings. From here there are two routes back to the village. One takes you along the top of the plateau, dropping sharply along a ruined temple and a palace. The other route takes you down a flight of steps to the riverbank, to the main ghats. There is a temple dedicated to Varaha that has twenty-four figures of Vishnu carved in green stone. There is also an 18-foot-long female figure of Chamundi that has ten arms holding clubs and skulls.

The major festivals celebrated here include Shivaratri (February/March) and Kartika Purnima (October/November).

KASHI VISHWANATH

Kashi Vishwanath temple houses one of the 12 Jyotirlingams. It is located in the city of Varanasi or Kashi as it was earlier called. An arch from the popular Dashashwamedha Ghat of Varanasi leads to the entrance of the eminent temple.

▲ **Shivalingam**

▲ The facade of Kashi Vishwanath Temple

Kashi Vishwanath Jyotirlingam Temple

The Kashi Vishwanath Jyotirlingam Temple in Varanasi is a small shrine built as recently as the late 18th century.

It was built by Ahilyabai Holkar, the Queen of Indore. A few years later, Maharaja Ranjit Singh, the Sikh ruler of Lahore, got the twin spires of the temple gold plated.

Nearby is the **Jnana Vapi Kupa** or 'the well of wisdom'. It is said, that in the wake of the demolition, the sacred Shivalingam in Kashi Vishwanath was hidden in this well till the present temple was built. Now the Jyotirlingam is set upon the floor inside a small sanctum within a silver square. Devotees offer milk, *Gangajal*, lotus flowers, garlands of *mandara* flowers and *dhatura*. They chant the name of Lord Shiva while offering all these to the Shivalingam.

The temple also has a number of other shrines dedicated to Vishnu, Avikukta Vinayaka, Dandapanishwara, Kal Bhairav and Virupaksha Gowri.

BAIDYANATH

▶ **Baidyanath Dhaam**

Deoghar is a small town in Jharkhand and is home to one of the 12 revered Jyotirlingams. It is mentioned in Shiva Purana that Ravana, the king of Lanka, was a great devotee of Lord Shiva. He wanted to take the Lord to his land. Lord Shiva told Ravana that he could take one of his 12 Jyotirlingams which would be as effective as his own presence. The only condition was that Ravana was not supposed to place the lingam anywhere on earth en route Lanka. Other gods did not want Ravana to take the lingam of Lord to the country of demons. As Ravana began his journey, the God of water, entered Ravana's stomach and Ravana had to descend to earth to relieve himself. Ravana, then, requested a Brahmin who was actually Lord Vishnu to hold the Jyotirlingam for a few minutes. Vishnu left the lingam on the spot and vanished. Ravana returned to find the Jyotirlingam firmly fixed on the ground. In his frustration, he pressed it with his thumb and tried to uproot it. The signs of his fingers can still be seen on the lingam. He could not carry the lingam to Lanka with him, so he came there every day to perform worship. This place came to be known as Baidyanath Dhaam.

Baidyanath Jyotirlingam Temple

There are 22 temples in the Baidyanath Jyotirlingam Temple complex. There are shrines of Parvati, Jagatjanani, Ganesha, Brahma, Sandhya, Kal Bhairav, Hanuman, Mansa (the serpent goddess), Annapurna, Lakshmi Narayana, Nilkantha, Nandi etc.

Among all these temples, the main temple of Shiva as Baidyanath is the most revered. Shiva presides here as a *Vaidya*, the physician.

▲ **Baidyanath Jyotirlingam Temple**

A golden pitcher shines bright at the crest of the temple. An extremely rare and precious moonstone is mounted on top of the crest from inside. It is said to have been brought by the demon king Ravana from Kuber's capital Alkapuri. It is believed that droplets of water kept falling on the Jyotirlingam from the moonstone even though there is no known source of water on top of the temple. Even today, these droplets can be seen falling.

The greatness of this temple lies in the fact that it is believed to have been erected by Vishwakarma (the engineer god).

In the north of the temple there is one holy pond known as **Shivaganga**. The old name of Shivaganga is Varvoghar kund. It is situated just 200 metres away from the Baidyanath Temple. It is believed that Ashwini Kumaras, the doctors of gods, bathed in this tank and cured themselves from diseases. Taking bath into this pond is considered same as taking bath into the holy Ganges.

KEDARESHWAR

This is one of the most sacred pilgrimage centres of the country, located in the lofty Himalayas. Kedarnath is a shrine steeped in antiquity and rich in legend and religious significance. It is located on the Rudra Himalayan range.

▲ **Shankara Samadhi**

Kedareshwar Jyotirlingam Temple

Located in the Himalayas, this small shrine is accessible only six months a year. The temple at Kedarnath enshrining the Jyotirlingam of Shiva opens only when the Sun enters the zodiac sign of Aries and it is closed when the Sun enters Scorpio. The priests then go to Ukhimath, where the worship of Kedareshwar is continued during the winter season.

Legend has it that Parvati worshipped Kedareshwar to unite with Shiva as *Ardhanareshwara*. Inside the Badrinath Jyotirlingam Temple, there is an irregular three-faced *lingam*, representing the hump of Lord Shiva when He took the form of a bull. The temple has three parts — the *garbhagriha*, the *darshan mandap* where *pujas* are conducted and the *sabha mandap* where devotees assemble. Outside the temple door, a massive stone idol of Nandi stands as a guard. There are deities of goddess Parvati and Ganesha in front of the main altar door. Outside the second door are the idols of Lord Krishna, the five Pandavas, their wife Draupadi and their mother Kunti. In the temple, there is a Lakshmi-Narayana deity, which was installed by Adi Shankaracharya.

This temple faces south, which is a unique feature, as traditionally temples face east.

▼ **Kedarnath Temple**

NAGESHWAR

Nageshwar is located between Dwarka and the Bet Dwarka islands, at the coast of Saurashtra in Gujarat. The Rudra Samhita refers to Nageshwar as Daarukaavane Naagesham.

▲ The statue of Nageshwar

Nageshwar Jyotirlingam Temple

Legend has it that a devotee by the name Supriya, was attacked by a demon Daaruka while in a boat. The demon imprisoned him along with several others at his capital Daarukaavana where he resided with his wife Daaruki. Shiva appeared in the form of a Jyotirlingam and vanquished the demon with the *Pashupat astram.* This Jyotirlingam manifestation is worshipped as **Nageshwar** at this shrine.

Nageshwar Jyotirlingam Temple is a lovely temple where the Lord revealed himself as a column of light. A huge attractive three-storey-high statue of Shiva as the meditating ascetic presides outside the temple. A patchy road traverses through flat lands to reach this well-maintained temple.

The Sivalingam in the temple faces south, while the *gopuram* faces east. There is a story behind this position. There was a devotee named Naamdev, who once started singing hymns in front of the *lingam*. Other devotees asked him to stand aside and not hide the Lord. To this Naamdev asked them to suggest one direction in which the Lord did not exist, so that he could stand there. The enraged devotees carried him and left him on the southern side. To their amazement, they found the *lingam* turn itself to the south with the *gopuram* still facing east.

This powerful Jyotirlingam is believed to give protection from all poisons. Thus it is said that those who pray to the Nageshwar *lingam* become free of poison.

▲ Nageshwar Temple

GHRISHNESHWAR

The temple of Ghrishneshwar is located near Aurangabad in Maharashtra. The temple stands on a bowl of flat land fringed by ancient basaltic hills in the distance.

Ghrishneshwar Jyotirlingam Temple

The *Shiva Purana* speaks of the emergence of the *lingam* at this place. It is believed that on Devagiri mountain there lived a Brahmin named Sudharma along with his wife Sudeha. He was a scholar of the Vedas, the scriptures and taught many students. The couple did not have a child of their own because of which Sudeha was sad. After much persuasion, she got her sister Ghrishna married to her husband. Ghrishna used to make 101 *lingams* daily and worship them. After the worship she would immerse them in the Ela Ganga River nearby. By the blessing of Lord Shiva, Ghrishna had a baby boy. Because of this Sudeha started feeling jealous of her sister. Out of jealousy, one night she killed Ghrishna's son and threw him in Ela Ganga where Ghrishna used to immerse the *lingams*. When Ghrishna discovered this, she did not even flinch and said, "He, who has given me this child shall protect him too." She started reciting "Shiva-Shiva" continuously. When she went to immerse the 101 Shiva*lingams* after prayers, she saw her son coming. Seeing her son she was neither happy nor sad. At that time, Lord Shiva appeared before her. Ghrishna prostrated before Shiva and requested to forgive Sudeha. She also requested him to appear at that place in her own name. Pleased with her, Lord Shiva manifested himself in the form of a Jyotir*lingam* and assumed the name Ghrishneshwar. The lake came to be known as Shivalaya thereafter.

The Ghrishneshwar Jyotirlingam Temple is compact and unassuming. The *sabha mandap* is supported by sixteen carved columns. A huge idol of Nandi faces the *lingam*. The *garbhagriha* is an underground chamber. At noon, the Ghrishneshwar temple turns magical when pink-turbaned musicians in the *nagaarkhana* launch into a *bhajan*. The strains of '*Om Jai Jagdish*' of pipe and drum fill the air as the priest rings his silver bell and swirls the sacred fire.

This temple is a fine example of medieval architecture and has some beautiful carvings. The temple is made of spotted red sandstone. It has some beautiful sculptures of Indian Gods including Brahma, Vishnu, Ganesh, the marriage of Shiva and Parvati, celestial beings, and even Maratha heroes. The beautiful and huge temple is still as fresh as it was when built. Worshippers of Lord Shiva flock to the temple from all over the country.

▲ **Ghrishneshwar Temple**

TRIAMBAKESHWAR

The town of Triambak (three eyes) is 30 kilometres west of Nasik. One of the 12 Jyotirlingams is here and close by is the source of the Godavari River. There is also an impressive Maratha Fort on the nearby hill.

▲ Triambakeshwar Temple

Triambakeshwar Jyotirlingam Temple

The three *lingams* in this 18th century temple dedicated to Triambakeshwar are eye-shaped. 'Tri' means three, and 'ambak' means eye, so *triambaka* means the 'three-eyed one', that is, Lord Shiva.

At Triambakeshwar Jyotirlingam Temple, the devotees enter from the south and approach the sanctum, a few steps below the main *mandap* (hall) of the temple. The Jyotirlingam is housed in a small depression inside. The water of Godavari constantly pours out of the top of the *lingam*. Usually the Shivalingam is covered with a silver mask.

Triambak is near the source of the Godavari, which is one of the most important holy rivers in India. The confluence of Godavari and its tributary Ahilya is just outside the Triambakeshwar Temple.

This place is known for lots of religious rituals. *Narayan-Nagbali, Kalsarpa Shanti, Tripindi vidhi* are performed here. *Narayan-Nagbali puja* is done at Triambakeshwar only. This *puja* is performed on three special dates. Some days are not suitable to perform this *puja*. This *puja* is performed for many reasons like to cure an illness, going through bad times, getting a child, and financial crisis.

The town of Triambakeshwar has a large number of Brahmin households and is also the centre for Vedic *gurukuls*. It also has many *ashrams* devoted to *Ashtanga Yoga* – the Hindu art of Living.

Kushavarta Teertha

It is said that this is the exact spot where the drop of ambrosia fell from the Kumbh vessel, for which Kumbh Mela is famous.

You have to walk up a flight of 690 steps to reach **Gangasagar**, a tank of water fed by the source of Godavari River. It is believed that the Ganga and Godavari emanate from the same source by an underground passage.

The round trip climb to **Brahmagiri**, the source of the Godavari, takes two or three hours. On the way you pass a temple dedicated to the goddess Ganga, a cave that has 108 Shivalingams, a temple dedicated to the sage Gautama whose ashram was said to be here, and the remains of the Anjeri Fort.

At a distance of twenty minutes from the Anjeri Fort is the **Gaumukha** Temple, where the source of the river Godavari is located.

RAMESHWAR

▲ Ramanathaswamy Temple

*The ocean at Rameshwaram is alluringly gentle, stretching away into the horizon as if it were a particularly large lake. The sunrise over **Agni Teertham**, the sacred stretch of shallow sea that is directly in front of the legendary Ramanathaswamy Temple is as it must have been when Lord Rama was here to offer prayers to Lord Shiva as a penance for killing Ravana, a Brahmin.*

Ramanathaswamy Jyotirlingam Temple

This temple is considered to be as old as the *Ramayana*. In keeping with the dimensions of this grand temple, the Nandi here is magnificently huge. The sanctum is embellished by beautifully carved granite pillars and guarded by handsome *dwarapalakas*. The *lingam* that Sita made while Hanuman could not reach on time is called Ramalingam and is worshipped in the main altar. To the right is the Vishwalingam brought by Hanuman. Among the two Shivalingams, Vishwalingam is worshipped first.

This sacred pilgrimage is considered complete if *Gangajal* brought from Varanasi is used for worshipping the *lingam*.

Since we have already covered this temple in *Chaar Dhaam* section, for further details and other information on the temple, please refer to Rameshwaram in *Chaar Dhaam* section on page 23.

▲ Ramanathaswamy Temple corrridors

BHIMASHANKAR

▶ **Bhimashankar Temple**

Bhimashankar Temple is situated in District Pune on the Sahayadri range, by the banks of the river Bhima. Bhima River flows from here.

Bhimashankar Jyotirlingam Temple

It is believed that Lord Shiva was pleased by the devotion of a demon called Tripurasura and granted him his wish for immortality at this spot. But the Lord added a condition that only the one who was a half-man and a half-woman could kill the demon. Tripurasura was overjoyed for he thought that such creature did not exist. He started terrorising the world. Parvati then entered Shiva's body and on the holy day of *Kartik Purnima*, killed the demon. It is said that Shiva's sweat fell on this place and became the sacred Bhima River.

Bhimashankar Jyotirlingam Temple has exquisite gold *kalash* and lavishly ornamented *shikhar*. Inside the temple, the Shivalingam is housed in an underground chamber that glows in the lamplight. Devotees circumambulate the *lingam*.

Just outside the *sabha mandap* is a small stone temple dedicated to Shani Maharaj. It features a stone idol of the God astride a Garuda, as well as a *panch dhaatu* bell. Two stone Nandi bulls are also present on this spot.

Bhimashankar Temple is surrounded on three sides by small shrines — **Rama Mandir**, **Dutt Mandir** and **Mataji ka Mandir**. From Dutt Mandir's roof, a clear view of *shikhar* and *kalash* at Bhimashankar Temple can be seen.

▲ **Bhimashankar Temple**

Guptabhima is a well-marked trail near the temple which leads to the place from where the River Bhima originates. Here the river swirls with terrifying force over a *lingam* which has been placed on a stone ledge.

The Bhimashankar Temple is a combination of both old and the new structures. Built in the Nagara style of architecture, it is a modest yet graceful temple which dates back to mid 18th century. The *shikhara* of the temple was constructed by Nana Phadnavis. The great Maratha ruler Shivaji is also believed to have made endowments to this temple to enable the carrying out of worship services. Similar to the other Shiva temples in this area, the sanctum is at a lower level.

Although the structure here is fairly new, the shrine Bhimashankaram and the Bhimarathi River have both been referred to in literature dating back to the 13th century.

▲ **Bells in Bhimashankar Temple**

PANCH SAROVAR

There are five holy lakes in India where taking a dip washes away your sins. These are collectively known as panch sarovar, and include Mansarovar, Pushkar, Bindu Sarovar, Narayan Sarovar and Pampa.

1. Mansarovar

This lake was created by Lord Brahma. Located at an approximate height of 15,000 feet, Lake Mansarovar holds deep spiritual influence and wide religious significance among the people of the trans-Himalayan region.

2. Pushkar

It is on the edge of the Rajasthan desert. There are over 400 temples in Pushkar. Some of the important temples are dedicated to Brahma, Raghunath, Varaha, Savitri, and Gayatri. Pushkar is famous for its annual Camel Fair which takes place in October/November.

▲ Skies reflected in Mansarovar Lake

3. Bindu Sarovar

It is located right next to the Lingaraja Temple, located in Bhubaneswar in the State of Orissa.

4. Narayan Sarovar

This lake surrounds the main Akshardham monument in Ahmedabad in Gujarat.

5. Pampa

It lies in the forests of the Western Ghats in the State of Kerala. Devotees take a dip in this river before proceeding to Ayyappa Temple.

MANSAROVAR

Hindus believe that by the purgation of soul in holy water, one can establish union with the Divine, and that a dip in Mansarovar provides with that celestial opportunity.

▲ **Mansarovar Gauri Kund**

The Mansarovar Lake lies towards the north of far western Himalayan and Tibet-bordering districts of Darchula and Humla in the Mahakali zone. Pure in beauty and tranquil in surrounding, the lake in the lap of Himalayas has remained a site of holy reverence for Hindus.

In Hinduism, the sanctity of the lake and its power of spiritual healing have been held high for ages. Circumambulating the lake and taking a dip in it is believed to purge one's soul from sins and the body from sickness. The site is also revered as the dwelling of the Divine which promises eternity to earthly creatures.

Several legends are related to Lake Mansarovar suggesting the miraculous power of healing.

Some say that by taking a dip in the lake, one can regain his youth, while the others opine that taking a dip in it helps one attain *moksha*. The lake is usually visited in rainy season because in winter, the snow-deep region is virtually impossible to reach.

The Lake Mansarovar, playing in the lap of the towering Himalayas, has a reference since Vedic times, in *Manas Khanda* of *Skanda Purana*. As described in *Skanda Purana*, Sage Dattatreya once went to the Himalayas where Lord Himalaya welcomed him and asked him for the reasons for ascending to the Himalaya Parbat. Dattatreya replied, "I want you

▲ **The divine Lake Mansarovar**

to take me to all the hidden pilgrimage sites in your lap." Hearing that, Himalaya took him to a site called Manas which was created by Brahma (the creator of the Universe). In those early times, Manas was the dwelling place of great sages and at the centre of *sarovar* (lake) there laid a golden Shivalingam. Dattatreya went around the lake and took a dip in it.

Why did Brahma create Mansarovar?

As narrated in the *Puranas*, it is believed that Brahma's son Marichi went to Kailash Parbat to catch a glimpse of Lord Shiva and Goddess Parvati. Together with many sages, he started worshipping Lord Shiva in his bid to please him. But, as winter came, the water in Kailash turned into snow with not even a single drop of water remaining anywhere. As they had to take a bath prior to commencing their rituals every day, Marichi, at his wit's end, invoked Brahma. When Brahma appeared, Marichi, together with the sages, implored him to help them cope with the problem. It was then that Brahma created Lake Mansarovar.

▲ **Lord Brahma**

▼ **Bathing in the blessed waters**

PUSHKAR

Pushkar is located 10 kilometres north-west of Ajmer and 400 kilometres south-west of Delhi. There are over 400 temples in Pushkar. Some of the important temples are dedicated to Brahma, Raghunath, Varaha, Savitri, and Gayatri. Pushkar is famous for the Camel Fair which takes place every year in October / November.

▲ Pushkar Lake

Pushkar Lake is considered as one of the most sacred spots. It is believed that one dip in the waters of this lake on *Kartik Purnima* is equivalent to performing *yajnas* for several hundred years. The charming lake amidst the hills has 52 bathing ghats built around it. The water around each ghat has special powers.

Naga Kund is believed to give fertility, **Roop Teertha** gives beauty and charm, **Kapil Vyapi Kund** helps in curing leprosy and **Mrikand Muni Kund** grants the boon of wisdom.

The other important ghats are the **Varaha Ghat** which is very sacred as Lord Vishnu is believed to have appeared here in the form of boar.

According to the *Padma Purana*, Brahma, the creator of the Universe, killed a demon named Vajranabha with a lotus flower. He dropped the lotus at this place to kill the demon. Petals fell at three spots where lakes emerged. These lakes are located within a radius of six miles. As Brahma threw the *pushpa* (flower) with his *kar* (hand), so the place got the name Pushkar. At **Gaya Kund**, near Pushkar, people offer *puja* (worship) for the salvation of their ancestors.

Temples

The **Brahma Temple** has a red tower and a *hans* (swan), the carrier of Lord Brahma over the doorway. In the temple, there is a deity of four-headed Brahma with Gayatri on his left. There are also deities of Indra and Kuber in the temple.

The **Varaha Temple** has a beautiful 2-foot-high white deity of Lord Varaha. Lord Varaha is said to have appeared in Pushkar. The original temple here was built in the 12th century.

There are two **Raghunath Temples** in Pushkar, the old and the new one. The deities in the new Raghunath Temple are Vaikunthanath and Lakshmi. The deities in the old Raghunath Temple, built in 1823, are Venugopal, Narasimha and Lakshmi.

▲ Ladies in traditional clothing at Pushkar Lake

The **Savitri Temple**, on top of Ratnagiri hill, almost on the outskirts of the town, is dedicated to Brahma's wife. The temple dates back 2000 years. It is a tough climb up an old stairway to reach this temple.

According to the *Pushkar Mahatmaya*, Brahma was performing a *yajna* at Pushkar. Both husband and wife had to sit in the *yajna*. Brahma's wife Savitri was asked to be present.

She was late in arriving. In her absence, reluctant to let the auspicious hour pass, Brahma married Gayatri, a local girl whom Indra found.

A hurt and enraged Savitri cursed her husband that he would not be worshipped at any other place on the earth. Consequently, Pushkar hosts the only Brahma Temple in India. Savitri also cursed Indra that he would not win any battle henceforth. She also cursed Vishnu who was present at Brahma's second marriage and had sanctioned it, to take rebirth as Rama and go through the suffering this incarnation entailed. She also cursed all the Brahmins present there that they would always stay poor. She then vowed to stay at a place where she would not even hear Brahma's name. That is why her temple is located atop Ratnagiri Hill which is a steep climb away from the Brahma temple. In the Brahma Temple, it is Gayatri, not Savitri, who sits with Brahma in his temple chamber.

Naga Hill

Naga Hill is considered one of the oldest hills in the world. On this hill is Naga Kund.

▼ Entrance to Brahma Temple, Pushkar

The story of this hill is that on the second day of the *yajna* performed by Brahma, Rishi Chyavan cursed Vatu, the grandson of Brahma, to become a snake. Vatu was cursed because at the *yajna*, he released a snake that coiled around Bhrigu Muni, the father of Rishi Chyavan. After Vatu begged for forgiveness, Brahma blessed him to live near this natural kund on Naga Hill. Agastya Muni is also believed to have lived in a cave on Naga Hill which is about 2 kilometres from Pushkar.

▲ The sculpture of Lord Brahma

▲ Horizon stretching beyond the Pushkar Lake

Pushkar Fair

The famous Pushkar Fair takes place from *Ekadashi* (11th day of the waxing phase of the moon) till *Purnima* (the full moon day) of *Kartik*. About 2,00,000 people come to the fair along with 50,000 camels, cows, and buffaloes. The reason why so many people come during this time is because it is considered a very auspicious time to bathe in the Pushkar Lake.

BINDU SAROVAR

▲ **Lord Parashurameshwara**

It is said that Lord Shiva established Bindu Sarovar as a place of pilgrimage by bringing water from all the holy places. Bindu Sarovar is located near Lingaraja Temple in Bhubaneswar. The deity of Lingaraja is brought to the pavilion in the middle of the lake and ritually bathed during the annual chariot festival (Ashokashtami). Most of the temples are located near the Bindu Sarovar Lake which is about 2 kilometres south of the city centre.

Lingaraja Temple

The presiding deity is the *swayambhu lingam* called Hari Hara *lingam*, which is half-Shiva and half-Vishnu. The deity is also named Tribhuvaneshwara, the Lord of the three worlds. The *lingam* of Lingaraja, or Krittivasas, is an uncarved block of granite 8 feet in diameter and raised 8 inches above the ground.

The Shivalingam is bathed daily with water, milk and *bhaang* (opium). There are many other deities in the temple.

In the north-east corner of the temple, there is a deity of Parvati. The main tower is 180 feet high.

According to the tradition, one should first visit this temple before going to *Puri*.

◄ **Mukteshwara Temple from outside**

There is a four-day-long chariot festival every March/April when Lingaraja is drawn on his chariot to the Rameshwara Temple. There is a 20-foot-high viewing platform along the northern wall of the temple and from this vantage point, you can get a good view of the temple compound.

Mukteshwara Temple

Built in the 10th century, this small elegant temple has been described as the most exquisitely ornamented temple in Bhubaneswar. It has a 35-foot-high tower. The sandstone carving is the most notable feature of this temple.

It is also known for its ornamental gateway and intricate motif carvings of a smiling lion, adorned with beaded tassels in its mouth. Mukteshwara means the Lord who bestows freedom through yoga.

Parashurameshwara Temple

This temple is the oldest Shiva Temple in Bhubaneswar. It was built in the late 7th century. There are many intricate carvings on this temple. It is on the east side of Bindu Sarovar and towards north-east of the Lingaraja temple. It has interesting carvings of elephant and horse processions and intricately carved windows. In the corner of the courtyard is the *Sahasralingam*, which is made of 1001 small *lingams* joined together.

▲ Ancient sculpture in Mukteshwara Temple

Brahmeshwara Temple

This temple, built around 1050, is a Shivalingam Temple. It is known for its intricately carved sculptures. It is at a walking distance from the Rajarani Temple. On the north wall of the porch is a carving of Goddess Lakshmi.

▲ Ancient art defined through sculpture

Rajarani Temple

The Rajarani Temple was built in 11th century. It is surrounded by a nice garden. Today this temple is no longer used for worship. This temple was dedicated to Lord Brahma and is known for its well-carved tower. Around the temple are carvings of the eight *dikpalas* (temple guards) who protect the temple from the different directions. They are eight important demi-gods namely **Indra** (east) the head of the demi-gods, **Agni** (south-east) god of fire, **Yamaraja** (south) god of death, **Nritti** (south-west), **Varuna** (west) god of water, **Vayu** (north-west) god of air, **Kuber** (north) god of wealth, and **Ishana** (north-east).

Vaital Devi Temple

This interesting 8th century temple is dedicated to Goddess Chamunda (Kali). She wears a necklace of skulls and is shown as the eight-armed slayer of the buffalo demon. Her necklace and the corpse she is sitting on, is usually hidden by her robes. In her arms she holds a snake, a bow, a shield, a trident, a thunderbolt and an arrow with which she is piercing the neck of the demon thus displaying the most terrifying aspect of the goddess Kali. This temple is close to Bindu Sarovar and has some intricate exterior carvings.

► Rajarani Temple

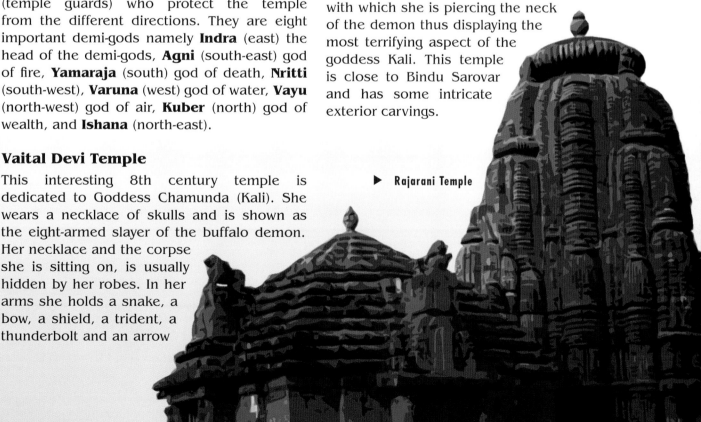

NARAYAN SAROVAR

From Vedic times, India had a glorious tradition of pilgrimage places in the form of rivers, stepwells and lakes. Following this tradition, a sacred water lake, Narayan Sarovar is located in Gujarat.

The lake surrounds the main Akshardham monument in Ahmedabad. It contains holy waters from 151 rivers and lakes, sanctified by Lord Swaminarayan. It also includes Mansarovar Lake in the Himalayas.

Surrounding the Narayan Sarovar are 108 *gaumukhs*, symbolising 108 names of God, from which holy water issues forth. Fully-bloomed lotus flowers in the lake impart an inspiring message of purity and detachment here.

Narayan Sarovar literally means the Lake of Narayan, another name of Vishnu. It is one of the most sacred pilgrimage sites of Hindus. The architecture is ancient and truly remarkable. Here, there are temples of Shri Trikamraiji, Laxminarayan, Govardhannathji, Dwarkanath, Adinarayan, Ranchodraiji and Laxmiji. These temples were built by Maharaj Shri Deshalji's queen. Devotees from all over India come to worship the lords here.

Akshardham Monument

The Akshardham Monument lies at the centre of the spacious Akshardham complex.

It is an architectural marvel comprising 10 imposing storeys entirely made of intricately carved 6000 tonnes of pink sandstone from Rajasthan, with no steel or cement used at all, ensuring the longevity of the monument. It is 108 feet tall and 131 feet wide.

Designed and crafted according to ancient Indian Architectural Treatises (called the *Sthapatya Shastras*), the monument radiates a spiritual aura into the complex and is drenched with silence and peace.

▲ The gaumukhs surrounding the Narayan Sarovar

PAMPA

*Pampa Surovar is in the forests of the Western Ghats in the State of Kerala. The **Sabarimala Ayyappa Temple** is located on a hill rising from this river. The temple is 4 kilometres north of Pampa Sarovar and the devotees take a dip in this sacred Sarovar before climbing up the hill.*

Ayyappa Temple

Ayyappa is said to be the son of Lord Shiva and Mohini (female form of Lord Vishnu). He is called Hariharaputra, the son *(putra)* of Vishnu *(Hari)* and Shiva *(Hara)*. He is also regarded as the third son of Shiva. He was abandoned on the banks of Pampa and found by King Rajashekhar of Pandalam. Ayyappa performed several miracles and once his father learnt of his divine origin, he decided to build a temple for his son.

The temple, built at the spot decided by Ayyappa himself, faces east. The main deity of Ayyappa is about one-and-a-half foot tall and is made of an alloy of five metals. There are images of Ganapati and Nagaraja in the south-west corner.

There are eighteen steps that lead to the temple and are regarded as a staircase to the heaven. To walk on these steps, the

▲ Sabarimala Ayyappa Temple

pilgrim must have observed forty-one days of penance and carried the *Irumudi* on his head. *Irumudi* is a cloth bag which has two compartments. The front portion contains a coconut filled with ghee along with camphor and other such things required for *puja* and the rear portion of the bag contains rice and other provisions for the journey. This bag is the only item that a pilgrim carries.

The pilgrims dress in the colours of renunciation, black or ochre clothes, wear a *rudraksha* or a *tulsi mala* (rosary), remain celibate, eat only vegetarian food, visit temples and worship for forty-one days before coming to this temple. Persons on this pilgrimage call each other swamy and chant *Swamiye, Saranam Ayyappa* (Lord Ayyappa, I surrender to you).

▲ The celestial Pampa Sarovar

SAPT SARITA

*Though the **Vedas** and **Puranas** mention more, but seven Indian rivers are considered the most sacred ones in our country. There are many temples on the banks of these rivers where people can go, take a holy dip and pray to get rid of their sins.*

1. Ganga

The holiest of all the rivers, Ganga or the Ganges is a perennial river, which is held in high regard by the Hindus. The river originates from Gaumukh in the Gangotri glacier right at the top of the Himalayas. A dip in Ganga is said to absolve all the sins.

2. Yamuna

Yamuna is also considered a sacred river in India. It originates from the Champasar Glacier in the Himalayan Mountains of Uttarakhand. A dip in Yamuna is believed to remove the fear of death.

3. Saraswati

There are numerous references to Saraswati River in ancient Indian literature. It is believed to have drained the north and north-west region of India.

4. Narmada

Narmada rises on the summit of Amarkantak Hill in Madhya Pradesh. It flows through many states before emptying into the Arabian Sea in Bharuch District of Gujarat.

5. Godavari

Godavari rises in the Western Ghats 80 kilometres from the Arabian Sea and flows eastward across the Deccan Plateau. Godavari is also a sacred river to Hindus.

6. Kaveri

Kaveri is also known as *Dakshin Ganga* because it flows in South and is as sacred in South India as Ganga in North India. Kaveri originates from Talakaveri in the Western Ghats in the State of Karnataka.

7. Sindhu

Sindhu River originates in the Tibetan plateau in the vicinity of Lake Mansarovar. This river runs its course through Jammu and Kashmir along the entire length of the country. It is one of the longest rivers in the world with the total length of 3200 kilometres.

GANGA

Ganga originates from Gaumukh in the Gangotri glacier drop by drop in trickles. Gaumukh is the snout of the Gangotri glacier, shaped like a cow's mouth. The Gangotri Glacier at the foothills of the Himalayas in north Uttarakhand is the source of Bhagirathi which joins with Alaknanda to form Ganga at the canyon-carved town of Dev Prayag.

▲ **The goddess Ganga**

The Ganga has an exalted position in the Hindu ethos. It is repeatedly mentioned in the *Vedas*, the *Puranas*, and the two Indian epics, the *Ramayana* and the *Mahabharata*. Ganga is a goddess, Ganga Devi, one of the two daughters of Meru (the Himalaya), the other being Uma, consort of Shiva.

According to the legend when the ruler of Ayodhya, King Sagar, performed the *Ashwamedh Yajna*, Indra kidnapped and hid the horse in the hermitage of the sage Kapila Muni. 60,000 sons of King Sagar came to the hermitage in search of the horse and mistaking Kapila Muni to be the abductor, attacked him. An enraged Kapila Muni burned all the princes to ashes. Later when King Sagar's grandson Anshuman begged the powerful sage to bring his family back to life, the sage advised the prince to bring the waters of the celestial river Ganga on earth to provide salvation to the souls of the dead princes.

King Bhagiratha, the great grandson of King Sagar, offered penance and prayers and goddess Ganga agreed to come to the earth. However, the might of the river was too much for the earth to withstand. Fearing a catastrophe, Bhagiratha prayed to Lord Shiva for help. Lord Shiva held out his matted hair to catch the river as she descended, and thus stopped the Ganga from flooding the earth.

Bhagiratha patiently led the river down to the sea from the mighty Himalayan Mountains.

During her course of journey, Ganga divided herself into a hundred mouths that form the Ganges delta. One of these streams washed the ashes, and provided salvation to the souls of the 60,000 dead princes of King Sagar.

The Ganga has many names associated with her many roles in Hindu mythology.

◀ **Ganga, the waterway to nirvana**

Bhagiratha himself is the source of the name **Bhagirathi**. While Bhagiratha led Ganga, then at one point, he went too close to the sage Jahnu's meditation site. The disturbed hermit immediately gulped down all the waters. Eventually, after much persuasion from Bhagiratha, the sage yielded the waters and Ganga got the name **Jahnavi**.

Water from the Ganga has the property that any water mixed with even the minutest quantity of Ganga water becomes Ganga water and inherits its healing and other holy properties. Also, despite its many impurities, Ganga water does not rot or stink if stored for several days.

From Dev Prayag to the Bay of Bengal and the vast Sundarbans Delta, the Ganga flows some 1,550 miles, passing and giving life to some of the most populous cities of India including Kanpur, Allahabad, Varanasi, Patna and Kolkata.

The **Yamuna**, which originates less than a hundred miles east of the Bhagirathi, flows parallel to the Ganga and a little to the south for most of its course before merging with the Ganga at the holy city of Allahabad, also known as *Triveni Sangam*, literally, three-way-junction, the third river being the mythical Saraswati which is supposed to be an underground river.

▲ Ceremony at Ganga Ghat

A large number of tributaries join and flow from the Ganga. The largest tributary to the Ganga is the **Ghaghara**, which meets it before Patna (Bihar) bearing much of the water from

▲ Goddess Ganga descending from heaven

Himalayan glacier in Northern Nepal. The **Gandak**, which comes from near Kathmandu, is another big Himalayan tributary. Other important rivers that merge with the Ganga are the **Son**, which originates in the hills of Madhya Pradesh, the **Gomati** which flows past Lucknow, and the **Chambal** made notorious by the ravines in its valley. The delta of the Ganga, is a vast ragged swamp forest called the **Sundarbans**, home of the Royal Bengal Tiger.

▲ Ganga in Rishikesh

SARITA-2

YAMUNA

▲ The revered Yamunotri

The Yamuna and the Ganga are considered the most sacred rivers in India. Yamuna, according to the legends, was the daughter of Surya (Sun God) and sister to Yama (God of Death). Consequently, it is believed that those who take a dip in holy waters of Yamuna are not tormented by the fear of death.

The river Yamuna is intimately connected to Lord Krishna's childhood pranks and miracles. New Delhi, the capital of India, and Agra, the site of the illustrious Taj Mahal, are the two major cities located on the banks of this river.

Originating from the Champasar Glacier in the Himalayan Mountains of Uttarakhand, the revered Yamuna flows down majestically through the verdant mountains and plains of north India. Some say the source of the river is the Saptarishi Kund, a glacial lake. There is a sacred shrine of Yamunotri near this source. At **Hanuman Chatti**, the Hanuman Ganga merges with Yamuna River.

The **Tons**, largest tributary of the Yamuna, has some beautiful spots in its upper reaches. Forests of Alder and Blue Pine lead to the famous Har-ki-Dun catchment area, source of another tributary, the **Rupin**.

Arising from the source, river Yamuna flows through a series of valleys for about 200 kilometres in lower Himalayas and emerges into Indo-Gangetic plains. In the upper stretch of 200 kilometres, it draws water from several major streams. The combined stream flows through the Shivalik range of hills of Himachal Pradesh and Uttarakhand states of India and enters the plains at **Dak Pathar** in Uttarakhand. From Dak Pathar, it flows through the famous Sikh religious place Paonta Sahib. Flowing through Paonta Sahib, it reaches Hathnikund/ Tajewala in Yamuna Nagar district of Haryana. It enters Delhi after traversing a route of about 224 kilometres.

The Yamuna, after receiving water through other important tributaries, joins the river Ganga and the underground Saraswati at Prayag in Allahabad at **Triveni Sangam**.

◀ Yamuna in Agra

SARASWATI

Saraswati River is believed to have drained the north and north-west region of India in ancient times supporting a large number of settlements. There are numerous references to this river in the ancient Indian literature.

▲ **A vedic manuscript**

Rig Veda, the most ancient of the four Vedas, describes Saraswati as a mighty river with many individually recognised tributaries. The sacred book names it as the seventh river of the Sindhu-Saraswati river system, hence the name Saptasindhu for the region bounded by river Saraswati in the east and Sindhu (Indus) in the west.

The *Saptasindhu* Rivers include **Saraswati**, Shatadru **(Sutlej)**, Vipasa **(Beas)**, Asikni **(Chenab)**, Parosni **(Ravi)**, Vitasta **(Jhelum)** and Sindhu **(Indus)**. Among these, the Saraswati and the Sindhu were major rivers that flowed from the mountains right up to the sea.

Saraswati is believed to have originated from the Har-ki-Dun glacier in Uttarakhand. It flowed parallel to the river Yamuna for some distance and later joined it, proceeding southwards as the Vedic Saraswati. The seasonal rivers and rivulets, including **Ghaggar**, joined Saraswati as it followed the course of the present river through Punjab and Haryana.

River Sutlej (the Vedic Shatadru) joined the river Saraswati as a tributary at Shatrana near Patiala. Saraswati, then, followed the course of Ghaggar through Rajasthan, Gujarat and Hakra in Bhawalpur before emptying into the Rann of Kutch via Nara in Sindh province, running parallel to the Indus River.

As of today, a part of the river exists as Ghaggar in Haryana; the rest of it has disappeared in the fringes of the desert of Rajasthan, Gujarat and Sindh. The perennial rivers Sutlej and Yamuna were once the tributaries of the Saraswati. It is believed that subsequently some tectonic movements may have forced the Sutlej and Yamuna to change their course and hence Saraswati dried up in a period spread over a few hundred years possibly between 2000 and 1500 BC.

▼ **Sarswati**

NARMADA

River Narmada is one of the most important sacred rivers of India. It is believed to have formed from the perspiration of Lord Shiva while performing the Tandava (cosmic dance).

Narmada rises on the summit of Amarkantak Hill in Madhya Pradesh and for the first 320 kilometres of its course winds among the Mandla Hills, which form the head of the Satpura Range. Then it moves through Jabalpur passing through the 'Marble Rocks'. Thereafter, it enters the Narmada Valley between the Vindhya and Satpura ranges and pursues a direct westerly course to the Gulf of Cambay. It flows through the states of Madhya Pradesh, Maharashtra and Gujarat. Further on, it empties into the Arabian Sea in the Bharuch District of Gujarat.

According to the *Skanda Purana*, Narmada is born of the white sweat that fell from Shiva's body. She, therefore, is considered to be his daughter.

The Narmada River is considered to be the giver of peace. Legend has it that the mere sight of this river is enough to cleanse one's soul, as against a dip in the Ganga. The Ganga is believed to visit this river once a year in the guise of a black cow to cleanse herself of all her collected sins.

There is the **Chaunsath Yogini** (sixty-four *yoginis*) Temple above the lower end of the Narmada gorge. The attendants of Durga are represented here. Although the images have been damaged, they still retain their pristine beauty.

Down the Narmada, there is a spectacular landscape with thickly forested mountain slopes, rocky regions with picturesque rapids, falls and whirlpools, and cultivated lands with rich black cotton soil.

Believed to have originated from the body of Shiva, the river is also known as *Jata Shankari*.

The worship of Shiva is common in these areas. Places along the banks — Omkareshwar, Maheshwar and Mahadeo — are all named after Shiva.

Omkareshwar has several old and new temples. There is an island on the river that is supposed to have one of India's twelve great Shivalingams.

Maheshwar is on the northern banks of the river. A fort and many temples are also located here.

◀ **Narmada River**

GODAVARI

Godavari rises in the Western Ghats 80 kilometres from the Arabian Sea and flows generally eastward across the Deccan Plateau, along the Maharashtra-Andhra Pradesh border and across Andhra Pradesh while turning south-eastward before reaching the Bay of Bengal. There it empties via its two mouths — the **Gautami Godavari** *to the north and the* **Vashishtha Godavari** *to the south.*

From its source to the Eastern Ghats, the Godavari River flows through gentle terrain, along the way receiving the **Darna**, **Purna**, **Manjra**, **Pranhita** and **Indravati** rivers. Upon entering the Eastern Ghats region, its width contracts until it flows through a deep cleft only 600 feet wide. Having passed through the Eastern Ghats, the river widens again, traversing the wide plains placidly till its confluence at Dhaulekharam in the Arabian Sea.

Legend associated with Godavari has it that Sage Gautama lived on the Brahmagiri Hills at Triambakeshwar with his wife Ahilya. The rishi kept his stock of rice in a granary. Once, a cow entered his granary and ate up the rice. When the rishi tried to ward the cow away with *durva* grass, it fell dead. The rishi wanted to relieve himself of the sin of 'Gauhatya'. He worshipped Lord Shiva and requested him to bring Ganga to purify his hermitage. Lord Shiva pleased with the rishi appeared as Triambaka and brought along the river Ganga. Since Ganga was brought down to Triambakeshwar by Sage Gautama, she is here known as Gautami. She is also known as Godavari because the river helped Sage Gautama to relieve him of his sin.

Nasik, being the city drained by this river, is known as an important centre of pilgrimage in India. Godavari is regarded as Deccan Ganga of Maharashtra. The sacred river Godavari going down from the Ahilyadevi Bridge takes a right angular turn to the south from the pious kund called Rama Kund.

The part of the town of Nasik, situated on the right bank of the Godavari, is known as **Shri Kshetra Panchavati**. Panchavati is a part of ancient forest area called Dandakaranya where Lord Rama, Lakshman and Sita lived during their exile. Kumbh Mela is held at Rama Kund every twelve years.

▼ Godavari River

KAVERI

*The Kaveri River is the smallest of the five major rivers of the Indian Deccan peninsula. The other four rivers are — Mahanadi, Godavari, Narmada and Krishna. However, it forms perhaps the most important watershed of the South. Kaveri is famous as **Dakshin Ganga** (the Ganges of the South). It serves as a lifeline to the people of Karnataka and Tamil Nadu.*

The Kaveri River basin is estimated to be 27,700 square miles with many tributaries including the Shimsha, the Hemavati River, the Arkavathy River, Honnuhole River, Lakshmana Tirtha River, Kabini River, Bhavani River, the Lokapavani River, the Noyyal River and the Amaravati River. Rising in southwestern Karnataka state, it flows southeast some 475 miles (765 kilometres) to enter the Bay of Bengal.

▼ **Kaveri, the Ganges of the South**

▲ **Kaveri Sangam Srirangapattam**

According to mythology, there was a childless king named Kaverna. Brahma gifted him with a beautiful girl named Kaveri. She was married to Sage Agastya on the condition that he would never leave her alone. One day, Agastya began teaching his disciples a difficult lesson in philosophy and got delayed in getting back home. Assuming that something unfortunate had happened to him and not wanting to live alone, she jumped into a tank. But she did not die. She became a river, and flowed down the Brahmagiri Mountain.

The river originates from Talakaveri in the Western Ghats in the State of Karnataka and flows generally south and east through Karnataka and Tamil Nadu across the southern Deccan Plateau through the south-eastern lowlands emptying into the Bay of Bengal. Its source is a spring in the Brahmagiri Mountains in Mysore. **Talakaveri** is a pilgrimage site set amidst Bramahagiri Hills in Kodagu.

The 765 kilometres long Kaveri River runs through some of the richest lands in South India watering the fields and blessing the people on its course. The people of Tamil Nadu celebrate the flood in a special way with a festival. This festival is called the 'Flood of the eighteenth'. On the eighteenth day of the month of *Aadi* (July/August), people worship the river. They light special lamps and express their gratitude by making offerings of fruits, sweetmeats and flowers to the river. It is a day of rejoicing for the people as they thank the river goddess for her blessings and prosperity.

SARITA-7

SINDHU

Originating from the Tibetan plateau in the vicinity of Lake Mansarovar, Sindhu River runs a course through Jammu and Kashmir towards the north along the entire length of country to merge into the Arabian Sea near Pakistan's port city Karachi. The total length of the river is 3200 kilometres.

▼ **Greenery mirrored in Sindhu River**

The river's name comes from Sanskrit word 'Sindhu'. It is mentioned in the *Rig Veda* and is the source of our country's name. Words like Hindu and Hindustan have been derived from *Sindhu* and the name India is derived from Indus, the name given to *Sindhu* by the foreigners.

A great Trans-Himalayan river, it is one of the longest rivers in the world. Rising in south-western Tibet, at an altitude of 16,000 feet, Sindhu enters the Indian Territory near Leh in Ladakh. After flowing towards Leh, Sindhu is joined on the left by its first tributary, the **Zanskar**, which helps turn the Zanskar Valley green. Many interesting mountain trails beckon the mountaineering enthusiasts to the Zanskar Valley. The Sindhu then flows past Batalik.

▲ **Sindhu making its way through the mountains in Leh**

The mighty Sindhu, when it enters the plains, is joined by its five famous tributaries — the **Jhelum**, **Chenab**, **Ravi**, **Beas** and **Sutlej** — giving Punjab the name 'Land of five rivers'.

There is a legend that Lord Buddha had graced Sindhu with his visit. Finding the climate extreme, and the area dry and dusty, he had permitted the *Bhikshuks* to wear shoes here. He had also permitted the use of padded clothing, forbidden elsewhere. To this day, historic Buddhist Stupas are found in Sindh.

The *Sindhu Darshan* or Sindhu Festival in Leh is celebrated in June. The festival aims at projecting the Sindhu as a symbol of India's unity and communal harmony. This festival is also a symbolic salute to the brave soldiers of India.

▼ **The facets of Zanskar Valley**

DIVYA DESAMS

The Divya Desams are 108 temples that are revered by Vaishnavite Hindus for special holiness. 106 of them are found on this earth while 2 are believed to exist in the spiritual realm. It is believed that 12 Alwars (the vaishnavite saint poets) visited 108 Vishnu temples and sang verses known as Pasurams.

Vaishnava Hindus, especially in South India, hope to visit the 106 Divya Desams that are here and wish to reach the God's feet in the rest 2 of the 108 Divya Desams, namely Thiruparkadal (the ocean of milk in which God resides) and Thiruparamapadam (at God's holy feet) located in divine lands.

The celestial Sri Padmanabhaswamy Temple in Thiruvananthapuram ▼

Andra Pradesh and North India

1. Thiruvengadam (Tirumala)
2. Ahobilam
3. Muktinath, Saligramam
4. Naimisaaranyam
5. Mathura
6. Gokul
7. Deva Prayakai
8. Thiruppirithi
9. Badrinath
10. Ayodhya
11. Dwarka

Kerala

12. Sri Padmanabhaswamy Temple, Thiruvananthapuram
13. Thiru Katkarai
14. Moozhik Kalam
15. Tiruvalla
16. Thirukadithanam
17. Sengunroor
18. Thiruppuliyoor
19. Thiruvaaranvilai
20. Thiru Vanvandoor
21. Thiru Naavaay
22. Viththuvakkodu

Tamil Nadu

23. Thirumeyyam
24. Thirukkottiyoor
25. Koodal Azhagar Temple
26. Azhagar Kovil (Near Madurai)
27. Tirumogoor
28. Srivilliputhur Andal Temple
29. Tiruththangal
30. Thiruppullani
31. Varadaraja Perumal Temple, Tirukkacchi
32. Ashtabhujakaram
33. Tiruvekkaa
34. Tiruththanka
35. Tiruvelukkai
36. Tirukalvanoor
37. Tiru Ooragam
38. Tiru Neeragam
39. Tiru Kaaragam
40. Tirukaarvaanam
41. Tiru Paramechura Vinnagaram
42. Tiru Pavala Vannam
43. Tiru Paadagam
44. Tiru Nilaaththingal Thundam, Ekambaranatha Temple

45. Tirupputkuzhi
46. Parthasarathy Kovil at Thiruvallikeni
47. Thiruneermalai
48. Thiruvidaventhai
49. Thirukadalmallai at Mahabalipuram
50. Bakthavatsala Perumal Temple at Thiruninravur
51. Veeraraghava Swami Temple
52. Thirukkadikai
53. Thiruvazhundhoor
54. Thiruindaloor
55. Kazhicsirama Vinnagaram
56. Thirukkavalampadi
57. Thiruchsempon Sey
58. Thiruarimeya Vinnagaram
59. Thiru Vanpurushoththamam
60. Thiruvaikundavinnagaram
61. Thirumanimadam
62. Thiruthevanartthogai
63. Thiruthetriyambalam
64. Thirumanikkoodam
65. Thiruvellakkulam
66. Thiruppaarththan Palli
67. Thalai Sanga Nanmathiyam
68. Thiruchsirupuliyoor
69. Thiru Vali Tirunagari
70. Thiruccithra Kootam
71. Thirukkan Nangudi
72. Thirunagai
73. Thiru Thanjai
74. Thirukkandiyoor
75. Thirukkoodaloor
76. Thiru Kavith Thalam
77. Thiru Adhanoor
78. Thiruppullam Boothangudi
79. Thirukkudandhai

80. Thiruccherai
81. Thiru Nandhipuravinnagaram
82. Thiru Naraiyoor
83. Thiruvinnagar
84. Thiruvelliyangudi
85. Thirukkannamangai
86. Thirukkkannapuram
87. Thiruvarangam
88. Thirukarambanoor
89. Thirukkozhi
90. Thiruanbil
91. Thiruppernagar
92. Thiruvellarai
93. Thirukkoilur
94. Thiruvayindhirapuram

95. Thiruvaramangai
96. Thirukkurungudi
97. Srivaikundam
98. Thiruvaragunamangai
99. Thiruppulingudi
100. Thirukkurugoor
101. Thirutthulaivillimangalam
102. Thirukkoloor
103. Thirukkulandhai
104. Thentirupperai
105. Thiruvattaru
106. Thiruvanparisaram

Moksham

107. Thiruparkadal
108. Thiruparamapadam

The five most important *Divya Desams* have been described here.

MUKTINATH TEMPLE

*Muktinath is one of the most revered Vishnu shrines located in Himalayas. The Hindus call the place as **Muktikshetra**, which literally means 'the place of salvation'. It is one of the 108 **Divya Desams**, the holy places of worship of Lord Vishnu, where the Alwars or Vaishnavite Saints had sung in praise of the Lord, which is compiled as the **Nalayira Divyaprabandam**.*

Muktinath is associated with the *shaligram*, the sacred stone worshipped by Hindus as Vishnu. Ancient legends refer to **Muktikshetra** as the region where salvation is attained and the source of the *shaligram*. It is also believed that Brahma performed a *yajna* here with Shiva and Vishnu as fire and water respectively.

Muktinath Temple is one of the most ancient Hindu temples of Lord Vishnu. It contains a human-sized copper idol of the God. There are images of Sri Devi and Bhu Devi on either side of the Vishnu idol. Next to the temple are 108 water-spouts. It is considered auspicious to bathe under the waters of the spouts.

Just below the temple of Muktinath is the eternal flame of **Jwala Devi Temple**. In this astonishing journey to Muktinath, you will find the only place on earth where you can find all *Panchtatvas*, the five elements out of which everything is made of — fire, water, sky, earth and air, at the same place together in their own distinct forms.

▲ **Jwala Devi Temple**

In addition to Lord Vishnu, Sri Devi and Bhu Devi, the temple also has the brass images of Goddess Saraswati, Garuda, Lava-Kusha and the *saptarishis*.

Muktinath is a sacred place for both Hindus and Buddhists. While Hindus call it Muktikshetra (the salvation valley), the Buddhists call it Valley Chumming Gyatsa, which in Tibetan language means the place of 108 waterspouts. It is believed that Guru Rimpoche (Padmasambhava), the founder of Tibetan Buddhism meditated here on his way to Tibet.

▲ **The facade of Muktinath Temple**

▲ **The towering Muktinath Temple**

VENKATESHWARA TEMPLE

*The Venkateshwara Temple is located in Tirupati town of Andhra Pradesh. It is dedicated to Sri Venkateshwara. The shrine is located on a hill at Tirumala, a cluster of seven hills known as **Venkatachalam**. Venkateshwara Temple is regarded as the richest temple of India. This temple also draws the highest number of devotees in the country.*

▲ **Lord Venkateshwara**

The temple at *Tirumala* is believed to have existed ever since the ancient times. The Tirupati Temple with its *gopuram* (tower) is a fine example of Dravidian architecture. The elaborate rituals and mode of worship in the temple prescribed by the Saint Ramanujacharya are followed even today. Anointing the idol with camphor and the offering of the hair by pilgrims by getting themselves shaven is an important custom at Tirupati Temple.

The *vimana* over the sanctum sanctorum is entirely plated with gold and is known as *Ananda Nilayam*. The shrine consists of three *prakarams* or enclosures. The outermost enclosure contains the

▶ **Golden sanctorum of Tirupati Tirumala Temple**

Dhwajastambha (flagpost). Others include the statues of Vijayanagar king, Krishna Deva Raya with his consorts and Todarmal, the minister of Akbar.

▲ **Gopuram of Tirupati Tirumala Temple**

The idol of the deity, the full figure of Lord Venkateshwara or 'Venkataramana' or 'Srinivasa' or 'Balaji', as it is called in various parts of the country, has the attributes of both Vishnu and Shiva — the preserving and destroying aspects of the Hindu Trinity.

Every day is a day of festivity at Tirupati Tirumala. The most famous is the annual festival called *Brahmotsavam* which is celebrated on grand scale for nine days in September. The fifth and the ninth days of the festival are very significant as *Garudotsavam* and *Rathotsavam* take place on those days.

The daily programme at Tirupati Tirumala Balaji Temple or the Venkateshwara Temple starts with *Suprabhatam* (wakening the Lord) at three in the morning and ends with the *Ekanta Seva* (putting the Lord to sleep) at one in the night. Daily, weekly and periodical *sevas* and *utsavams* are performed to the Lord. Interested pilgrims choose from the list and pay to get the *sevas* or *utsavams* done in their name.

PADMANABHASWAMY TEMPLE

Thiruvananthapuram is a city dominated by temples. Padmanabhaswamy Temple located here is an ancient temple and the city of Thiruvananthapuram derives its name from the name of the presiding deity enshrined in the temple.

The temple is one of the most important 108 *Divya Desams*, the holy abodes of Lord Vishnu. The temple's main deity Padmanabhaswamy is a form of Vishnu in *Ananantashayanam* posture depicting the eternal sleep of *yoga nidra*.

In the temple, Mahavishnu lying on his five-headed serpent *sheshnag* is an image of divine power. The majestic black idol is made of 12008 *shaligrams* bound by a mortar of jaggery and other substances. The idol is seen through three separate openings for *darshan* of the feet, the navel with the lotus emerging from it and the face. Brahma is seated on the lotus rising from Vishnu's navel and a Shivalingam is sheltered by Vishnu's right hand.

Outside the south door of the temple is a shrine for the small but fearsome Narasimha, which is considered to be highly potent. The entrance

▲ An idol displayed during Painkuni Festival at Padmanabhaswamy Temple

▲ Padmanabhaswamy Temple from outside

corridors of the temple, the *sivelipura* and the 1000-pillared hall have high roofs supported on sculpted granite pillars.

The evening *deeparadhana* (lighting of lamps) is a sight to behold. Around 6:30 p.m. people gather at the *Abhishravana Mandap* as priests light the lamps around the idol until the flames reflecting off the pillars turn the air into liquid gold.

RANGANATHASWAMY TEMPLE

This temple is the largest one in India and one of the largest religious complexes in the world. The temple is enclosed by seven concentric walls enclosed by twenty-one gopurams. Among the marvels of the temple is a hall of 1000 pillars. The presiding deity is Lord Ranganatha. Apart from the main shrine of Ranganatha, the complex also houses shrines of various forms of Lord Vishnu, including Sudarshana Chakra, Narasimha and Rama.

According to *Sriranga Mahathmiyam*, Lord Brahma was once in a state of deep meditation; and in his supreme trance, he got the gift of the Lord Vishnu's idol, *Ranga Vimana*. The idol was then passed over by Brahma to Viraja, Vaiswatha, Manu and Ishwaku, and then finally descended to Rama. Lord Rama, himself an *avatar* of Vishnu, gifted it to King Vibhishana as a token of appreciation for his support against his own brother, Ravana.

Though Vibhishana supported Rama, he was basically a demon, and hence the *Devas* did not want a demon taking Lord's supreme form to his kingdom. They requested Lord Vinayaka to help them. Vibhishana, while on the way back to his kingdom, passed through Trichy.

He wanted to take a bath in the river Kaveri and do his daily rituals. However, he was perplexed as the idol once placed on land could never be removed and had to be in that place forever. Suddenly, he saw Lord Vinayaka standing there in the disguise of a cowherd boy. Vibhishana asked him to hold the idol till he came back. As per the plan, when Vibhishana was bathing, Lord Vinayaka kept the idol firmly on the sand on the banks of Kaveri. On seeing this, angry Vibhishana chased him but the boy climbed over the rock near the Kaveri bank.

Vibhishana finally caught the boy and hit him on his forehead, who then revealed himself to be Lord Vinayaka. Vibhishana immediately apologised and the Lord gave him his blessings after which Vibhishana continued on his way to Lanka.

The place where the Ranganathan idol was kept was later covered in deep forests and after a very long time, it was discovered when a Chola king chasing a parrot found the idol accidentally. He then established the Ranganathaswamy Temple. The rock to which Vinayaka ran from Vibhishana now forms the famous temple of **Uchi Pillayar Kovil**.

◀ **The Ranganathaswamy Temple**

VARAHALAKSHMINARASIMHA TEMPLE

Varahalakshminarasimha Temple is located in Simhachalam in the state of Andhra Pradesh. Simhachalam is a small pilgrimage centre which has the most famous, rich and best-sculpted temple dedicated to Narasimhaswamy.

▲ Varahalakshminarasimha Temple

Varahalakshminarasimha Temple is a sacred *Divya Desam* which soars atop the hill. This temple has *ugra* (fiery) God who embodies himself as not one but two *avatars* (incarnations) of Vishnu. This temple uniquely represents both Varaha (the boar) and Narasimha (the man-lion) incarnations of Vishnu.

According to a legend, King Pururva was riding over the hills on his *Pushpak Vimana* with his spouse Urvashi. His *vimana* was drawn towards Simhachalam by some magical force. Here the king found the idol of God as he had seen in his dream. The Lord ordained that the idol was to be exposed to view only on the *Tritiya* (third day) of the bright half of the month of *Vaishakha*. For the rest of the year, the idol is covered with sandalwood paste.

Only on *Vaishakha Shuddha Tritiya*, the worship is offered to the Lord's *nijaswarupa* (true form).

A thousand steps lead to the temple from the foot of Simhachalam hill. The front *gopuram* of

▲ Ancient sculpture of Lord Narasimha

▲ Ancient Lord Varaha

the temple is decorated with figures of gods and goddesses.

This is the most impressive feature of Varahalakshminarasimha Temple. Covered in sandalwood paste, the deity can be seen in resplendent *nityaswarupa* (daily form).

The *Kappa Stambha*, a pillar to the left of the sanctum is decorated with bells and silk cloth. Embracing the pillar is believed to bless childless couples with offsprings. It is said that a *Sanatana Gopala Yantra* has been placed under it. On the southern wall of the sanctum, a standing image of Lord Narasimha is shown tearing open the demon Hiranyakashipu. **Puttukoppulu** is the place where devotees get their hair tonsured. **Gangadhara** is a small stream west of the temple where pilgrims have a bath.

SHAKTI PEETHA

▲ Lord Shiva with his consort Parvati

Ma Kali ▶

The Shakti Peethas are the places where Shakti, the female form of power is worshipped. They are sprinkled throughout the Indian subcontinent. This goddess is often associated with Parvati, the goddess of marital felicity, and with Durga, the goddess of strength and valour.

According to *Puranas*, King Daksha performed a *yajna*, to which he invited all the Gods except his son-in-law, Lord Shiva. Daksha's daughter Sati, though uninvited, went to attend the *yajna*. At the venue, she found her father speaking ill of her husband. In anger, she immolated herself and died. Lord Shiva's *ganas*, on hearing this news, killed Daksha and destroyed the *yajna*. Lord Shiva himself in deep anguish picked up the lifeless body of Sati and roamed around all the three *lokas* doing *tandava* dance.

Lord Vishnu, fearing that Shiva's *tandava* might destroy the entire Universe, sent his *chakra* to cut Sati's body into pieces. Wherever the pieces of her body and jewellery fell, a form of *Shakti* manifested. Hence, these places came to be known as Shakti Peethas. At all Shakti Peethas, the goddess *Shakti* is accompanied by Lord Bhairava, a manifestation of Lord Shiva. According to *Mahapitha Purana*, there are 51 such Shakti Peethas.

▲ The dancing Shiva

Ma Durga killing a demon ▶

SL. No.	Place	Body Parts and Ornaments	Form of Shakti	Related Bhairava
1.	Hingula, Pakistan	The suture on the top of the head (Brahmarandhra)	Kottawisha (Bhairavi)	Bhimlochan
2.	Sharkrar, Kolhapur	Three eyes	Mahishasuramardini	Krodheesh
3.	Sugandha	Nose	Sunanda	Triambak
4.	Amarnath Cave, Kashmir	Throat	Mahamaya	Trisandhyeshwar
5.	Jwalamukhi, Kangra, Himachal Pradesh	Tongue	Sidhida (Jwalamukhi Devi)	Unmatt Bhairava
6.	Jalandhar	Left breast	Tripurmalini	Bheeshan
7.	Baidyanath	Heart	Jai Durga	Baidyanath
8.	Nepal	Both the knees	Guhyeshwari Mahamaya	Kapal Bhairava
9.	Manas	Right palm	Dakshayani	Amar
10.	Utkal Virja, Jagannath Puri	Umbilical cord	Vimla	Jagannath
11.	Muktinath, Nepal	Right cheek	Gandaki	Chakrapani
12.	Katwa, Veerbhum, West Bengal	Left arm	Bahula Devi	Bheeruk
13.	Ujjaini, Madhya Pradesh	Elbow	Mangal Chandika	Kapilambar
14.	Tripura	Right leg	Tripur Sundari	Tripuresh
15.	Chatgaon, Bangladesh	Right arm	Bhawani	Chandrashekhar
16.	Shalbadi Gram, Jalpaigudi	Left leg	Bhramari	Ishwar Bhairava
17.	Kamgiri, Assam	Genital organ	Kamakhya	Umanand
18.	Prayag, Allahabad, Uttar Pradesh	Right hand finger	Lalita	Bhav Bhairava
19.	Jayantia Hills, Assam	Left thigh	Jayanti	Kramdeeshwar
20.	Ksheer Gram, Bardhwan	Right hand thumb	Bhootdhatri	Ksheerkhandak
21	Kalighat, Kolkata, West Bengal	Right leg fingers	Kalika	Nakuleesh
22.	Lalbagh Court, Howrah	Diadem	Vimla	Samvart
23.	Varanasi, Uttar Pradesh	Earrings	Vishalakshi Manikarni	Kaal Bhairava
24.	Kanyashram	Back	Sarwani	Nimish
25.	Kurukshetra, Haryana	Right ankle	Savitri	Sthanu

SL. No.	Place	Body Parts and Ornaments	Form of Shakti	Related Bhairava
26.	Pushkar, Rajasthan	Both the wrists	Gayatri	Sarvanand
27.	Mallikarjun Hills, Shail	Neck	Mahalakshmi	Shambaranand
28.	Kanchi	Bone	Devgarbha	Ruru
29.	Kalmadhav	Left hip	Kali	Asitang
30.	Amarkantak, Madhya Pradesh	Right hip	Narmada	Bhadrasen
31.	Ramagiri, Chitrakoot	Right breast	Shivani	Chand Bhairava
32.	Vrindavan, Uttar Pradesh	Hair	Uma	Bhootesh
33.	Shuchi, Kanniyakumari, Tamil Nadu	Upper teeth	Narayani	Samhar
34.	Panch Sagar	Lower teeth	Varahi	Maharudra
35.	Kartoyatat, Bangladesh	Sole of the left foot	Aparna	Vaman Bhairava
36.	Shri Parvat, Ladakh	Sole of the right foot	Shree Sundari	Sundaranand
37.	Vibhash, Tamluk, West Bengal	Left ankle	Kapalini	Sarvanand
38.	Prabhas, Girnar Hills	Stomach	Chandrbhaga	Vakratund
39.	Bhairav Parvat, Ujjain	Upper lip	Avanti	Lambkarna
40	Panchavati, Nasik, Maharashtra	Chin	Bhramri	Vriktaksh
41.	Patna, Bihar	Right thigh	Sarvanandkari	Vyomkesh
42.	Godavaritir	Left cheek	Viveshi	Dandpani
43.	Ratnavali, Chennai	Right shoulder	Kumari	Shiv
44.	Mithila, Bihar	Left shoulder	Uma	Mahodar
45.	Vairat, Rajasthan	Toes	Ambika	Amrit
46.	Karnat	Ear	Jai Durga	Abhiru
47.	Vakreshwar	Part of brain	Mahishmardini	Vakranath
48.	Yashohar, Bangladesh	Left palm	Yashoreshwari	Chand
49.	Attahas, Labhpur, West Bengal	Lower lip	Phullara	Vishwesh
50.	Nandipur, West Bengal	Necklace	Nandini	Nandikeshwar
51.	Lanka	Anklet	Indrakshi	Raksheshwar

In this book, we have described the seven most popular Shakti Peethas.

MAHALAKSHMI (KOLHAPUR)

▲ The deity of Mahalakshmi

Kolhapur is located in Maharashtra and is well-connected with Pune. It is situated on the banks of the Panchganga River and is full of ancient temples and shrines. It is said that Sati's eyes fell at this place while Shiva was carrying her body around.

Legend has it that Kolhasura, a demon that tormented the Gods and other beings, was destroyed by Mahalakshmi here at Karavira, and that the spot of his death became a *teertha*. Mahalakshmi took abode here in a shrine which constitutes the temple today.

The *Mahadwara* (main entrance) of the Mahalakshmi Temple is the western entrance. Upon entering, one is confronted with several *deepamalas* on either side. Then comes the *Garuda Mandap* with square pillars and foliated arches of wood. An image of Garuda faces the sanctum. Another stone *mandap*, on a raised platform enshrining Ganesha, also faces the sanctum. Following this is the *mandap* with three shrines facing west. The central one is that of Mahalakshmi whose silver *naga* hood and gold crown and feet grow resplendently. The other two on either side are those of Mahakali and Mahasaraswati.

The image of Mahalakshmi carved in black stone is 3 feet in height. The *Shri Yantra* is carved on one of the walls in the temple. The sanctum is designed such that once a year, the setting rays of the Sun fall on the face of the image of Mahalakshmi for a period of three days. Above the Mahalakshmi sanctum is a shrine with Shivalingam and

▲ Mahalakshmi Temple, Kolhapur

▲ The Navagrahas—Surya, Chandra, Mangala, Budha, Brihaspati, Shukra, Shani, Rahu, Ketu

Nandi. There is another shrine with Venkatesh, Katyayani and Gauri Shankar facing the north, east and the south respectively.

There are a number of smaller shrines in the courtyard belonging to the Navagrahas, Surya, Mahishasuramardini, Vitthal, Shiva, Vishnu, Tulja Bhavani and others. Also located in the courtyard is the temple tank called **Manikarnika Kund**, on whose bank, a shrine of Vishweshwar Mahadev is located. The temple complex exhibits mortarless construction echoing the style of the early Deccan temples.

The worship is offered here five times a day. Each Friday and on full moon days, a festival image of the deity is taken out in procession around the temple courtyard.

AMBAJI (GUJARAT)

▶ **Ma Durga**

The Ambaji or Ambika Shakti Peetha is located at Arasur near Mount Abu in the south-west of the Aravalli hills in northern Gujarat. The river Saraswati originates from here and disappears into the desert of Kutch. Also located here is the Koteshwar Mahadev shrine.

Following the destruction of Daksha's sacrifice and the Rudra Tandava of Shiva, when parts of Sati's body fell at several places which are now revered as Shakti Peethas, the left breast of Sati is believed to have fallen at Ambaji. There is no idol of Ambika here, there is only a *Yantra*. Shakti here is Durga, the consort of Shiva.

Legend has it that Krishna worshipped Shiva and Ambika at Ambikavana and Rukmini worshipped Ambika here prior to her marriage with Krishna. Legend also has it that the tonsure ceremony of Krishna as the child was performed at Ambaji. Mount Abu

or Arbuda is associated with Vashishtha and is believed to be the place of his hermitage. Nandini, Vashishtha's cow is said to have fallen into a pit when river Saraswati came to her rescue. It is believed that river Saraswati filled the pit with water to enable the cow to come out.

The three main Shakti Peethas of Gujarat are **Ambaji** at Arasur, **Bala** at Chunval and **Kali** at Pavagadh near Champaner. Other Shakti shrines in Gujarat are those at **Asapura** in Kutch, **Arbudadevi** in Mount Abu, **Sundari** at Halvad, **Harsiddhi** at Kolgiri or Koyla and **Anasuya** on the Narmada.

MANGALA GAURI (GAYA)

▶ **Mangala Gauri**

This is a shrine dedicated to Shakti or the Mother Goddess in the predominantly Vaishnavite pilgrimage centre of Gaya. Mangala Gauri is worshipped as the Goddess of benevolence. The Mangala Gauri Temple is a Shakti Peetha where it is believed that the breast of Shakti fell. Shakti, here is worshipped in the form of a symbol of nourishment.

Mangala Gauri in Gaya has been mentioned in *Padma Purana, Vayu Purana* and *Agni Purana* and in other scriptures and *tantrik* works. The

▲ **A bird's eye view of Gaya**

present temple dates back to 1459 AD. It is a small brick temple facing east, built on top of the Mangala Gauri hill.

A flight of steps and a motorable road lead to the temple. The sanctum houses the symbol of the Goddess and it also has some finely carved ancient sculptures. A small hall or *mandap* stands in front of the temple. The courtyard also houses a fire-pit for the *yajna* or *homa*.

There are two minor shrines dedicated to Shiva and deities of Mahishasuramardini Durga and Dakshina Kali.

KUMARI (KANNIYAKUMARI)

Kanniyakumari is located at the southern tip of the Indian subcontinent. The small temple dedicated to Kanniyakumari is on the seashore, in the town known by the same name. Kanniyakumari is also the place where the spiritual leader Swami Vivekananda spent days in meditation upon a rock off the coast. It is said that Sati's back fell over here.

Legend has it that the demon Banasura wreaked havoc on the inhabitants of this world. It was then that Lord Vishnu told the Gods and the humans to request *Parashakti* (primeval energy) to vanquish the demon. Answering the prayers of the oppressed, *Shakti* appeared as a young virgin girl in Kanniyakumari and commenced penance with the desire of marrying Shiva. Sage Narada fixed the midnight hour as the auspicious time for the wedding.

When Shiva's procession reached a place called Vazhukumparai, a rooster crowed, heralding daybreak and Shiva, assuming that the auspicious hour has passed, returned back. The disappointed Goddess decided to spend her life in Kanniyakumari as a virgin. The demon Banasura upon hearing Shakti's story proceeded to Kanniyakumari to win her hand in marriage by force and this led to a fierce battle in which he was slain by her.

The black stone image of Kanniyakumari in the sanctum bearing a garland is an enchanting one. Of particular significance is the glittering nose ring that is visible from a distance.

There are also shrines of Vijayasundari and Balasundari who were the playmates of the Goddess in her youthful days.

The Vaishakha festival is celebrated here in which an image of the Goddess is taken around the town in procession on various mounts. The eastern door to the shrine is opened during the chariot festival. This door is also opened during Navaratri.

An image of the deity is held in worship at the *Navaratri mandap* throughout the duration of Navaratri, and processions mark the festive celebrations on each of the nine nights. The destruction of demon Banasur is enacted on Vijaya Dashmi, the concluding day of the Navaratri festival, when an image of the deity is taken in procession on a horse mount.

◀ Sun-drenched waters surrounding Vivekananda Rock Memorial in Kanniyakumari

▲ Navaratri mandapam in
  Kanniyakumari

KALIGHAT (WEST BENGAL)

▶ **Ma Kali**

Kalighat is located in the city of Kolkata on the banks of the River Hoogly (Bhagirathi). The original name of the city Calcutta is said to have been derived from the word Kalighat. Kali is regarded as one of the principal deities in Bengal.

Kalighat is one of the 51 Shakti Peethas of India, wherein various parts of Sati's body are said to have fallen in the course of Shiva's *Rudra Tandava*. Kalighat represents the site where Sati's toes of the right foot fell.

Kali is regarded as the destroyer or liberator and is depicted in a fearful form. Despite the terrifying form, she is considered to deliver bliss to worshippers. The Kalighat Temple attracts numerous devotees throughout the year.

Legend has it that a devotee discovered a luminous ray of light coming from the Bhagirathi riverbed, and upon investigating its source came upon a piece of stone carved in the form of a human toe. He also found a *Swayambhu lingam* of Nakuleshwar Bhairava nearby, and started worshipping Kali in the midst of a thick jungle. This shrine grew to its present form over a period of time.

The **Dakshineshwar Kali Temple** across the river, near Belur Math, bears an image of Kali worshipped by the spiritual leader Ramakrishna Paramahamsa who was the guru of Swami Vivekananda.

▼ **Kalighat Temple**

BHAVANI (MAHARASHTRA)

Worship of the primeval energy (Shakti) in the form of the Mother Goddess is seen in the four Shakti Peethas of Maharashtra, Tuljapur enshrining Bhavani, Kolhapur enshrining Mahalakshmi, Mahur enshrining Mahamaya, and Renuka and Saptshringi enshrining Jagadamba. Sati's right arm is believed to have fallen at this place.

Bhavani was the deity of Maharaja Shivaji, the valiant Maratha ruler, and is held in great reverence Maharashtra. Bhavani is considered to be an embodiment of ferocity, as well as *Karunaswaroopini* (filled with mercy).

▲ **Goddess Bhavani**

The Bhavani Temple in Tuljapur is located on a hill known as Yamunachala on the slopes of the Sahayadri range in Maharashtra near Sholapur. The temple entrance is at an elevation and visitors need to transcend a flight of steps to reach the shrine.

Bhavani is worshipped in the form of a 3-foot-high granite image with eight arms holding weapons, bearing the head of the slain demon Mahishasura. Bhavani is also known as Tulaja, Turaja, Tvarita and Amba.

Legend has it that Matanga demon wreaked havoc upon the *Devas* and the humans, who then approached Brahma for help. Upon his advice, they turned to the Mother Goddess Shakti, who took up the form of the destroyer, and vanquished him to enable the peace to reign again.

Legend also has it that Bhavani vanquished another demon that had taken the form of a wild buffalo (*Mahisha*), and took abode on the Yamunachala hill, which is now home to the temple.

The festivals of significance here are Gudi Padva in the month of *Chaitra*, Shriral Sashti, Lalita Panchami, Makar Sankranti and Rathasaptami. The deity is taken out in procession on Tuesdays. Navaratri is also celebrated with great fanfare. It culminates in Vijaya Dashmi.

KAMAKHYA (ASSAM)

The Kamakhya Temple in Assam is one of the most venerated Shakti shrines in India. Kamakhya is located on a hill called Neelachala Parbat or Kamagiri hill near the city of Guwahati in Assam.

Shakti, residing on the Kamagiri hill is known as Kamakhya, the one who grants all wishes. Traditionally, Assam has been known as the *Kamarupa Desha* and has been associated with *tantrik* practices and *Shakti* worship. According to the legends, following the destruction of Daksha's sacrifice and the *Rudra Tandava* of Shiva, the sex organ (*yoni*) of Sati fell here.

It is also believed that the supreme creative power of Brahma was challenged by *Shakti*, the Mother Goddess, and that Brahma could thereafter create, only with the blessings of the *yoni*, as the sole creative principle. After much penance, Brahma brought down a luminous body of light from space and placed it within the *yoni* circle, which was created by the Goddess and placed at Kamarupa.

The temple has a beehive-like *shikhar*. Some of the sculptured panels here hold great interest among the pilgrims and other tourists.

There are images of Ganesha, Chamundeshwari, dancing figures, etc. There is no image of *Shakti* here.

Within a corner of a cave in the temple, there is a sculptured image of the *yoni* of the Goddess, which is an object of reverence. A natural spring keeps the stone moist. Kamakhya temple was destroyed in early 16th century, and then rebuilt in the 17th century by King Nara Narayana. Images of the King and related inscriptions are seen in the temple.

Durga Puja is celebrated annually during Navaratri in the month of September/October.

▲ **Kamakhya Temple**

A unique festival observed here is the Ambubasi fertility festival wherein it is believed that the Goddess (Mother Earth) undergoes her menstrual periods. During this period, the temple is closed for three days and opened with great festivity on the fourth day. It is believed to be inauspicious to till the ground or to plant seeds, during these three days.

Many creatures, like tortoises, monkeys, and large number of pigeons have made the temple their home. They loiter around the premise, being fed by the temple authorities and the visitors. An ambience marked by ambiguity as well as the peace soothes the nerves of visitors, and takes their minds to flights of inner salvation. In fact, most of the people come here for this very reason itself.

With all its enigmatic splendour and picturesque locale, the Kamakhya Temple is one of the most amazing structures, not only in Assam, but also in the whole of India.

YATRAS

Yatra is a spiritual journey to a place of pilgrimage in a group. Travelling in a group is believed to be the most effective way of supporting yourself through these new experiences. Some of the important yatras undertaken with full devotion by the pilgrims in India are discussed here.

1. Kailash-Mansarovar Yatra

The Mansarovar-Mount Kailash region is a living shrine and one of the greatest and the most difficult to reach of all the places of pilgrimage. This is the most complicated *yatra* to Mansarovar Lake and Mount Kailash, the holiest lake and mountain respectively.

2. Amarnath Yatra

The annual Amarnath Yatra in the State of Jammu and Kashmir strides through an exceptionally enchanting route to meet the shining glory of God. After the *yatra*, each *yatri* has a tale to narrate about how the *yatra* changed his life.

3. Panch Kedar Yatra

Panch Kedar refers to the five temples of Lord Shiva in the high Himalayas. The five temples are Kedarnath, Madhyamaheshwar, Tungnath, Kalpeshwar and Rudranath. This *yatra* is characterised by the simplicity of its temples and rituals.

4. Vaishno Devi Yatra

The holy cave of Vaishno Devi is located in the folds of three mountains called Trikuta in Himalayas. The devotion and faith of the pilgrims of Vaishno Devi stems from their belief that *Mata* knows what is best for them.

5. Sabarimala Yatra

This *yatra* takes place in Kerala towards Ayyappa Temple located on a hill rising from Pampa Sarovar. There are two kinds of pilgrims to Sabarimala — one kind goes to the hill for a simple *darshan* and the other kind, the *Ayyappa Swamy*, begin their journey forty-one days beforehand.

6. Alandi-Pandharpur Yatra

This is the *yatra* undertaken by people in groups called *vari* to Vitthal Temple in Maharashtra. There are no caste, gender or class barriers to become a *varkari* (pilgrim) on this *yatra*.

▲ Towards Mansarovar

KAILASH-MANSAROVAR YATRA

Mount Kailash is considered the holiest mountain on earth. Lord Shiva resides here among the peaceful Himalayas. Among the thousands of deities of Hinduism, Lord Shiva finds a great place in the heart of all devotees. He is also called Bhola Baba because of his simplicity and readiness to grant whatever the devotee asks for.

A mythological story says that Lord Shiva once built a house for himself but gave it away to a devotee who asked for it. Thus he settled in the mountain of Kailash. This is his abode where he stays with his entire family including his wife Goddess Parvati and children Ganesha and Kartikeya and the other Shiva *Ganas*.

According to ancient religious texts, the abode of Lord Vishnu is called *Vaikuntha*, the abode of Lord Brahma is called *Brahmaloka* and the

abode of Lord Shiva is called *Kailash*. Of the three, Kailash is the only place where one can go bodily and return back.

A journey to Kailash-Mansarovar is considered as once in a lifetime achievement. Monks, *yogis* and pilgrims from all over the world have braved unimaginable hardships to reach this abode of gods. Its exceptional isolation and the peculiar contours of black granite that give it the appearance of a Shivalingam, have made

Kailash a sacred mountain which is respected as a place that is representative of Shiva.

Lake Mansarovar, as we have already discussed, is believed to have been created by Brahma. Pilgrims believe that in the dead of night, divine beings descend from the heavens to have a holy dip in the lake. A single dip washes away the sins of a lifetime.

Gauri Kund is the highest freshwater lake in the world. It lies just after Dolma La which is the highest point in Kailash *Parikrama*. The waters in Gauri Kund are frozen for the major part of the year and are credited with great powers of fertility for women.

Mount Kailash and Lake Mansarovar are situated in Tibet. Travellers who visit this place get the opportunity to experience spiritual traditions, and visit temples and monasteries, lakes and rivers, and mighty snow-clad peaks.

Kailash-Mansarovar Yatra has a few treks. The *yatris* have different options to choose from to reach Kailash-Mansarovar.

- By road from Nepal via Kodari
- By air to Lhasa and then by road
- By air to Simikot via Kathmandu and Nepalganj

▼ **Mount Kailash, the abode of Lord Shiva**

▲   Devotees performing puja

The Yatra

The Kailash-Mansarovar Yatra commences with arrival in Kathmandu — the capital city of Nepal where deities mingle with the mankind. A visit to the **Pashupatinath Temple** and other equally enchanting shrines is a perfect starting point for this spiritual journey.

The next stop is Zhangmu after crossing the China-Nepal border. It is a bustling town with a strong Chinese military presence. The next stop is the Tibetan town called Nyalam. A long day's drive to Saga introduces you to the beautiful world of nature in all its finery. Shishmapangma Peak stands majestically like a gentle, snowy dinosaur. En route you also get to see the enormous, turquoise blue Peigatso Lake.

From Saga, you can drive along the Yarlung Tsampo River towards Prayang. On the horizon are the Nanda Devi and other mountains in the Himalayan range.

As you drive from Prayang to Mansarovar, you come across Mayum Pass and Mayumla Lake. The contours of Gurla Mandhata Mountain tower over the horizon as you descend towards the Lake Mansarovar. Mount Kailash looms like an enormous, benign force field. Here begins the Mansarovar and Kailash *Parikrama* which include visit to **Gauri Kund**, **Rakshas Tal**, **Dolma La** and **Shiva Sthal**.

Parikrama of Mansarovar includes the trek from Hor Qu to Trugo, and from Trugo to Zaidi and Chiu, eventually leading to Lagna Gompa. After completing the Mansarovar *Parikrama*, you are ready for the Kailash *Parikarama* which has the trek from Darchen, Tarpoche, Deraphuk and Dolma La to Zutulphuk and then back to Darchen.

The return journey is retracing the steps back and after a long journey of almost a month, you finally return back to where you started — Kathmandu.

▼ Sacred waters of Mansarovar Lake

AMARNATH YATRA

The Amarnath Cave is situated on the narrow openings between the mountains of Lidder Valley. It is at a height of 13,700 feet above sea level in Jammu and Kashmir. The holy cave is 130 feet high. The cave is surrounded by snow-clad mountains. Shiva is worshipped here in the form of Shivalingam-shaped ice block made by the drops of water oozing naturally inside the cave.

▲ Amarnath Shivalingam

The *Lingams*

Most of the year, the cave is covered with snow. Only for a short period of time during summer this place is accessible for pilgrims. On the full moon day, in the month of August, thousands of pilgrims visit Amarnath Cave. At that time, the ice Shivalingam reaches its maximum size. Behind an iron fence with an open gate, an underground trickle of water emerges 10 feet up from a small cleft in the rock and freezes. It drops to form a tall, smooth cone of ice. Water droplets trickle slowly from the top of the cave and freeze into ice as they fall. First a solid base is formed, and then the *lingam* gets formed.

The *lingam* is formed of an ice stalagmite that waxes and wanes with the moon's circle. By its side, there are two more ice *lingams* considered to be those of Shiva's consort Goddess Parvati and their son Ganesha. The cave faces the south. Inside Amarnath cave, there is a small cave towards the left from which a chalk-like substance is given to pilgrims as *vibhuti*.

The Amarnath Cave

The legend surrounding the Amarnath Cave is that when Parvati insisted on knowing the secret of immortality and creation of the Universe, Shiva agreed to tell her the secret at a secluded place where no one could listen to it. He chose Amarnath Cave. In preparation to that, Shiva left his Nandi Bull at **Pahalgam**. At **Chandanwari**, he released moon from his hair. At the banks of **Lake Sheshnag**, he released the snakes. He decided to leave his son Ganesha at **Mahaguna Parbat**. At **Panchtarni**, Shiva left the Five Elements behind (Earth, Water, Air, Fire and Space), because he is the Lord of these elements.

Then, he took *samadhi* on the deer skin and began to concentrate. To ensure that no living being is able to hear the Amar Katha, he created a Rudra named Kalagni and ordered him to spread fire to destroy every living thing in and around the Holy Cave. After this, he started narrating the secret of immortality to Parvati. But as a matter of chance, one egg which was lying beneath the deer skin remained protected. The pair of pigeons which were born out of this egg became immortal having listened to the secret of immortality (*Amar Katha*). Many pilgrims report seeing the pair of pigeons when they trek the arduous route to the ice *lingam* at Amarnath.

▼ Mountains near Amarnath Cave

The Yatra

The *yatra* to Amarnath begins from Pahalgam from where Amarnath is 45 kilometres. From Pahalgam, the trek is on an ancient route. The confluence of the rivers Sheshnag and Lidder is located at Pahalgam. The 45 kilometres trek is covered in four days.

The first major stop is at Chandanwari where the rivers of Asthanmarg and Sheshnag meet.

Then comes Sheshnag, a mountain that derives its name from its seven peaks resembling the seven heads. From here one climbs to Pissu Top. Here the Gods are believed to have crushed the demons. Further up is the Sheshnag Lake.

Then one begins the steep climb to Mahaguna Pass at a height of 14,000 feet. The route to Mahaguna is full of rivulets, waterfalls and springs. From here, there is a downward slope leading to Panchatarni, a meadow at a height of 12,000 feet. Then finally one reaches Amarnath.

Taxis and jeeps go up to Chandanwari but from here it is a trekking route. Ponies are also

◄ Journey to Amarnath

► Entering the Amarnath Cave

available here to take the pilgrims. Alongside the Lidder stream, the trek is through a narrow lane. But from the top of the Pissu Hill, the ascending trek is comparatively smooth till Sheshnag. The Mahaguna Pass after Sheshnag is the highest point on the trek.

From here till Panchatarni, it is a downward slope. From here it is a 6 kilometres ascent to Amarnath Cave. This is the traditional route.

The new route via Batal is only 15 kilometres long. But the road here is narrow and *kuchcha* as compared to the traditional route. There are also steep rises and falls as compared to Chandanwari route. This route can be covered in one day. The two routes meet at a place called Sangam that is 4 kilometres short of the holy cave.

◄ **The long queue of pilgrims**

▶ **Beauty merged with piety**

PANCH KEDAR YATRA

Journey to Panch Kedar is one of the most difficult pilgrimages in India. Panch Kedar refers to the five temples of Lord Shiva in the high Himalayas — Kedarnath, Madhyamaheshwar, Tungnath, Kalpeshwar and Rudranath.

It is believed that the Pandavas, after their victory in the Mahabharata war, wished to pay homage to Lord Shiva. At Kedarnath, seeing the Pandavas coming, Lord Shiva disguised himself as a bull. However, the Pandavas saw through his disguise. Realising that the disguise had not worked, the bull tried to thrust itself into the ground. Bhima tried to hold the bull to prevent it from vanishing.

In the struggle, Shiva in the form of a bull got torn into separate parts. The forehead appeared at **Pashupatinath** in Kathmandu, the hump at **Kedarnath**, the torso and the navel at **Madhyamaheshwar**, the arms at **Tungnath** and the face manifested itself at **Rudranath**. The legendary matted locks of Shiva fell at **Kalpeshwar**. The five sites in India are referred to as Panch Kedars.

1. Kedarnath

Here the hump of Lord Shiva is worshipped. The trek to Kedarnath from Gauri Kund is along the river Mandakini. The Kattyuri-style temple is built with extremely large, heavy and evenly cut grey slabs of stones and has a wooden ceiling topped with gold *kalash*.

2. Madhyamaheshwar

Here the *nabhi* or middle part of Lord Shiva is worshipped. It is 21 kilometres from Ukhimath and is at a higher altitude than Kedarnath. The temple is located 25 kilometres north-east of Guptakashi. There is a motorable route from Guptakashi to Kalimath. From Kalimath it is a trekking route. The outer courtyard of the temple has an idol of Nandi bull and a small shrine of Shiva and Parvati. In the sanctum sanctorum, a brass Nandi bull is present along with the representation of the torso of Shiva.

3. Tungnath

Bahu or arm of Shiva is worshipped here. It is on the way to Badrinath at a distance of 37 kilometres from Ukhimath. This is the highest Hindu shrine in the Himalayas. The *swayambhu lingam* is 1 foot high, dark and tilting towards the left. Two smaller temples dedicated to Goddess Parvati and Vyas are found in a small courtyard.

Ravana, the demon king, is said to have performed penance at this temple. In the *Garbha Griha* the images of Shankar, Pandavas, Kal Bhairav, Ved Vyas and many others are seen.

4. Kalpeshwar

Jata or hair of the head of the buffalo-Shiva is worshipped here. Shiva is worshipped here as *Jatadhar*. It is located in Urgam valley. A black Nandi bull smeared with vermillion is placed near the gate of the temple. A small shrine of Hanuman is also there. To the right of the main temple is an idol of Ganesha. The main temple has the locks of Shiva in the shape of a protruding rock.

5. Rudranath

Mukh or face of the buffalo-Shiva is worshipped here. The temple is a small hut-like structure made of stones. Inside is the *swayambhu lingam* which represents the face of Shiva. While doing the *parikrama* of the deity, one has to sit and move at the section in the back. To the extreme left of the temple are six smaller temples with Shivalingams and a temple with several tiers of Shivalingams with burning *diyas*. To the right of the main temple is a small temple with a black idol. In an alcove to the left is a miniature Saraswati in white marble.

▲ Tungnath Temple

▲ Front view of Kedarnath Temple

▼ Kedarnath Temple from outside

The Yatra

The Panch Kedar Yatra begins with the shrine of Kedarnath. Then comes Madhyamaheshwar. To reach there, you go to Ransi Village. A gentle climb through pine forest brings you to Bantoli. From Bantoli you climb to Maikhamba Chatti. Madhyamaheshwar is 2 kilometres ahead.

The third stop is Tungnath. The stupendous views of the Nanda Devi, Bandarpoonch, Kedarnath, Neelkanth and Chaukhamba peaks are spectacular. The fourth stop in the Yatra is Kalpeshwar.

Rudranath is the most difficult of all five Kedars. It is a rough trek of 23 kilometres from Gopeshwar. One has to walk 18 kilometres to the temple on foot over high ridges. There are many holy Kunds near the Rudranath Temple namely **Surya Kund**, **Chandra Kund**, **Tara Kund**, **Manas Kund** and so on. It is believed that at Vaitarani River, the river of salvation, which is near this place, the souls of the dead cross when changing the world. Devotees come here to offer rituals to their dead ones.

▼ **Devotees at Kedarnath**

VAISHNO DEVI YATRA

▲ **Vaishno Devi**

The holy cave-shrine of Vaishno Devi is located in a beautiful recess of the Trikuta Mountains forming a part of the lower Himalayas in Jammu and Kashmir. The journey takes you through awesome wilderness amidst snow-capped mountains and sprawling forests to the shrine, sacred and mystical. It is believed that a supernatural power seems to draw pilgrims across the mountains as they climb those great heights chanting **'Jai Mata di '**.

▲ **Inside Vaishno Devi Temple**

As legend goes, Vaishno Devi, a devotee of Lord Vishnu had taken a vow of celibacy. Bhairon Nath, a *tantrik*, when saw her going towards the Trikuta Mountains, decided to chase her. The Goddess, feeling thirsty at Banganga, shot an arrow into the earth from where water gushed out. Charan Paduka, marked by the imprints of her feet, is the place where she rested. The Goddess then meditated in the cave at **Ardhakuwari**. This cave is called **Garbha Joon**. It took Bhairon Nath nine months to locate her. She kept Veer and Langur on guard outside the cave and asked them not to allow Bhairon to enter the cave. When Bhairon Nath tried to force an entry to the cave, Veer-Langur offered resistance and a terrific battle started. Vaishno Devi blasted an opening at the other end of the cave with her trident when Bhairon located her. Thereafter Devi took the form of Goddess Chandi and beheaded Bhairon Nath, whose skull was flung up the mountain by the force of the blow and fell at a place now known as **Bhairon Ghati**. Beheaded Bhairon now prayed to *Mata* for mercy and was granted a boon of liberation. She said, "My devotees will visit your place after they have come to me for darshan." A temple has been constructed at the spot where Bhairon's head fell. Accordingly, the pilgrims visit **Bhairon Temple** after offering prayers at *Mata's* cave.

▲ **Vaishno Devi Temple**

The Cave

Inside the cave, there are three natural *pindis* of Goddess Saraswati, Lakshmi and Kali which represent the creative, preservative and destructive aspects of the divine energy images of three deities. The holy Ganga's cold and crystal clear water washes the lotus feet of the *Mata's pindis*. Previously the shrine had only one natural entry cave, but now two more exit caves have been constructed.

The Yatra

Vaishno Devi Yatra begins at Katra. Then comes a small bridge under which River Banganga flows. About one-and-a-half kilometre away from Banganga River is the **Charan Paduka**. Then you reach Ardhakuwari. From there you reach Garbha Joon where *Mata* meditated in a cave. The entire 13 kilometres route is quite wide and tiled. Besides, the whole path is lit up every night by powerful sodium vapour lamps. After you reach **Bhavan** then on the right you see the holy cave. After crossing the cave the pilgrims walk through a corridor. Further down is a broad platform upon which a life-sized idol of the *Mata* has been enshrined. At the end of the tunnel three *pindis* of Kali, Saraswati and Lakshmi are kept. Outside the cave's exit is **Amrit Kund**. The next stop is the Bhairon Temple which is a steep climb from here.

SABARIMALA YATRA

Sabarimala is the best known pilgrimage destination in Kerala. It is situated high up in the Sahyadri Mountains. The temple attracts pilgrims not only from the southern states of India, but also from all over the world.

▲ **Lord Ayyappa**

Ayyappa's Birth

The most commonly believed story of Ayyappa's birth is that Shiva, struck by the beauty of Vishnu, asked him to take the female form. Ayyappa was born of this union. The child was abandoned on the banks of the River Pampa and found by King Rajashekhara of Pandalam. He named him Manikanda because he had a golden bell tied around his neck. Manikanda performed several miracles. When King Rajashekhara came to know of his divine status, he decided to build a temple for him. Manikanda shot an arrow into the hills to mark the spot where it should stand. He also specified that the temple should have eighteen steps representing the eighteen hills that he protects.

Ayyappa Temple

Ayyappa Temple is slightly sunken in a plateau at the top of the hill. It faces east. There are images of Ganapati and Nagaraja in the south-west corner. On the east side of the temple are the 18 sacred steps.

The golden youth Ayyappa is seated in the pose of a hermit with his hand in the *Chin Mudra* touching the thumb to the forefinger signifying the oneness of the devotee and the deity.

Mala and Irumudi

Mala and *Irumudi* are the two indispensable things carried by a pilgrim who goes on Sabarimala Yatra as 'Ayyappa Swamy'.

A pilgrim or Ayyappa Swamy who wishes to wear the *mala* and go to Sabarimala is initiated by a Guru Swamy (one who has been to Sabarimala before). On an

▲ **A sadhu in Sabarimala**

auspicious day, Ayyappa Swamy receives the string of *rudraksha* beads (*mala*) from Guru Swamy following a special *puja*. Now Ayyappa Swamy or the pilgrim has to live a life of ascetic till the yatra commences.

At the start of the journey, the Guru Swamy places a specially prepared two-part bundle called *Irumudi* on Ayyappa Swamy's head. The bundle holds offerings for Ayyappa, Malikapuram Devi and Vavar. The most important item in the bundle is a hollowed-out coconut filled with ghee. It is to be used for *abhishekam* at Sabarimala.

The Yatra

Pilgrims, who wish to go to Sabarimala, traditionally go in groups. The 4 kilometres climb from Pampa to the Sannidhanam takes an hour. The pilgrims stop at the **Saramkutti** where the young Ayyappa's arrow is said to have landed. When the pilgrims reach the eighteen sacred eastern steps of the shrine, they break fresh coconuts at the base and climb up to the **Sannidhanam**.

They open their bundle and sort out the offerings. The sealed coconuts are now broken and the *ghee* is offered for *abhishekam*. It is believed that by this gesture the pilgrims break their ego.

After *abhishekam*, the Ayyappa Swamys descend the eighteen sacred steps backwards while keeping their faces turned towards the Lord.

Those pilgrims who do not have the *Irumudi* are not called Ayyappa Swamy. They do not climb the eighteen sacred steps. Instead they turn to the right and come up the north steps. Once all the devotees have seen Lord Ayyappa, they move along towards the Ganapati and Nagaraja shrines.

Just after the *darshan* of Ayyappa, the pilgrims visit the **Malikapuram Devi Temple** and offer a cloth to the Goddess. The Goddess is considered Ayyappa's *Shakti* and also a manifestation of Madurai Goddess Meenakshi.

Pilgrims next offer dried fruits and nuts to Vavar in a doorless shrine containing a sword. This shrine is right next to the eighteen sacred steps. Vavar is said to be a pirate who was defeated by Ayyappa in a fight. Later on he became his devotee.

▲ Trees worshipping the holy Pampa River

Mandala Makara Vilakku Festival

Sabarimala, the abode of Lord Ayyappa, is exemplar of communal harmony. During the Mandala Makara Vilakku Festival, thousands of devotees, from all over the country come to offer prayer to the Lord irrespective of their religion and caste.

Mandala Makara Vilakku Festival season begins on November 17, with a customary function at 5:30 p.m. In this function, the chief priest, commonly known as *melshanthi*, opens the sanctum sanctorum of the temple and lights the ritual lamps in front of the Ayyappa idol. Millions of devotees visit Sabarimala during the annual pilgrimage, which usually begins in December and culminates by the middle of January.

Many pilgrims stay back till this festival is over, after which *Kuruthi puja* (offering of water mixed with *chunnambu* and turmeric powder to the forest deities) is performed.

Other Festivals

Onam, Mandalapuja, Pankuni Uthram (Lord's birthday) and Vishu are the other festivals celebrated at Sabarimala with pomp and glory.

▲ A devotee with offerings

ALANDI-PANDHARPUR YATRA

▲ An idol of Vitthal after the vari

A sea of people is gathered on the banks of River Indrayani under a grey monsoon sky. A miraculous silence reigns over the congregation. Around two lakh pairs of eyes stare at the saffron flag hoisted atop the temple at Alandi where Sant Gyaneshwar's padukas are kept. After some long minutes, a priest comes out and declares that Sant Gyaneshwar is set to begin his yearly journey to Pandharpur. "Palki Prasthan..." he announces. Soon all the voices join in chanting "Gyanba Tukaram...!" and the vari begins.

Home to Vitthal Temple

Pandharpur is a town located in the district of Solapur in Maharashtra in Western India. Alandi-Pandharpur is one of the most hallowed pilgrimage sites not only in Maharashtra, but in the whole of India. It is situated on the banks of the Bhima River, which is also known as Chandrabhaga, as it appears like a crescent moon. Chandrabhaga is now known as Chenab and is in Jammu and Kashmir. Alandi-Pandharpur is the home to the famous Vithoba or **Vitthal Temple**. Vitthal (Vithoba) is considered to be another name of Lord Krishna. Vitthal's consort in the temple is Rukmini.

The worship of Vitthal at Alandi-Pandharpur is derived mainly from the *puranas* and has been amplified by the contribution of the great Vaishnavite saints of Maharashtra and Karnataka.

▲ Inside the temple

Vari and Dindi

In Marathi, *vari* means a journey one must do again and again. Thousands of *varkaris* (devotees) gather at different venues and walk towards one destination — Pandharpur, the abode of Lord Vitthal in Maharashtra. For over a millennium, little has changed in Asia's biggest pilgrimage on foot, the Alandi-Pandharpur Yatra.

The *vari* is an eight-century-old tradition that traces its origins to Sant Gyaneshwar. The *vari* is a procession, which carries forth the *padukas* representing the four saints — Gyaneshwar, Namdeo, Tukaram and Eknath — to Lord Vitthal's temple in Pandharpur.

▲ Idol at Alandi-Pandharpur Vitthal Temple

In a *vari*, a *dindi* is a group of *varkaris*. All the *dindi*s in the *vari* are given numbers and they have to follow a certain prefixed walking order either ahead or behind the *palki* vehicle.

The *dindi* is convenient for *varkaris*. The collective rations, clothing and first-aid medicines are carried along with the *dindi* in a bullock-cart. Most of them arrange for a water tanker common to two to three *dindi*s. The walking schedule and plans of the halt are meticulously worked out by the *dindi* chiefs. Every *dindi* has a group of skilled performers. There are informal *vari* gatherings on the way and folk songs, dances and comic acts are presented.

All *dindi*s gather at their *palki* camp during evening *arati*. As the *palki* chief raises his baton, silence falls almost magically.

The *padshiche varkari* (those who carry necessities in a sack) do not belong to any *dindi*. They choose to do the *yatra* by carrying their own food and take shelter at temples or under big trees. Rarely does one see them today. The villages where the *varkaris* halt welcome them with some special delicacy. Most towns and villages en route arrange for free medical aid, accommodation and subsidised food.

Vitthal Temple

Vitthal Temple is about 2000 years old. The black sandstone idols of Vitthal and Rukmini are truly enchanting. During the *vari*, the temple remains open for 24 hours as the God is believed to remain awake for his devotees. After the *vari* is over, the temple is washed with water and the idols are given a different diet of spices and sugar and a new set of clothes as they are said to be tired after a hectic day. Both the idols wear an exquisite array of jewellery.

Pundalik Temple

According to the legend, Pundalik was an ardent devotee of Lord Vitthal, also known as Vithoba. He always considered the service of his parents higher than to that of God. Once, he ordered the gurgling Bhima River not to disturb his sleeping parents. Delighted by his devotion, Vishnu granted him a boon, and the river calmed down. Till date, this river is placid and flows silently as Chandrabhaga in Pandharpur. On appearing at Pundalik's doorstep, Lord Vitthal found Pundalik with his parents sleeping with their heads in his lap. So as not to offend the Lord, Pundalik presented a brick to the Lord. Even today, Lord Vittal can be seen standing on that brick, still waiting to be entertained by his devotee, at Pandharpur.

The Pundalik Temple is just opposite to the Vitthal Temple. The fisherfolk or *kolis* manage this temple. Outside this temple is a small stone boat – 3 feet by 2 feet, but it is too heavy to be lifted with bare hands. However when it is placed in the water, it actually floats.

▲ **An ancient sculpture of Lord Vishnu and Lakshmi**

The Yatra

Over 150 *palkis* (palanquins in which the *padukas* are carried) start from different destinations in western and southern India. Accompanying the *vari* are the *varkaris* who walk from villages in Andhra Pradesh, Tamil Nadu, Karnataka, Gujarat and Maharashtra. Some walk for over two months, while for the others, the journey takes about ten days to three weeks. These days, thousands of *varkaris* reach Pandharpur directly in buses or other vehicles, but the charm of the *vari* lies in performing the Yatra on foot.

The routes of the Sant Gyaneshwar *palki* and the Sant Tukaram *palki* have remained the same over the centuries. Sant Gyaneshwar *palki* starts from Alandi and reaches Pandharpur via Lonand, Phaltan and Velapur. The Sant Tukaram *palki* reaches Pandharpur via Sholapur.

There is no fixed date on which the *vari* must begin, but the concluding day is fixed. *Varkaris* from different places draw up a walking schedule so that they reach Pandharpur on the auspicious day of *Ashadhi Ekadashi* in July.

Varkaris coming from all directions meet at the holy city of Pandharpur. The entire night before *Ashadhi Ekadashi*, the pilgrims sit on the banks of River Chandrabhaga.

At the crack of dawn, after taking a dip in the chilly waters of the Chandrabhaga, the pilgrims proceed to the Vitthal Temple barefoot. The beats of the *mridanga* follow them. In a moment, the flag on the crown of the temple comes into sight and, like a miracle, all the *varkaris* bend down on their knees to pay homage to their beloved Lord Vithoba. The most unforgettable moment is when they behold the jet-black, beautifully decorated idol of Vithoba at Vitthal Temple.

Ringan and Dhava

Vari traditions are unique and beautiful. The *ringan*, a human chain, is an exciting contest in which a sacred horse called *Maulincha Ashva*, believed to be the soul of the saint whose *palki* is being carried, runs through the rows of *varkaris*, who try to catch even the tiny soil particles kicked off by the horse's hooves. Different types of *ringans* are performed at several spots on the way to Pandharpur.

In Marathi, *dhava* means to run. It is said that Sant Tukaram caught the first glimpse of the Vitthal temple at Pandharpur while standing on a hillock near Velapur and he started running downhill in sheer exhilaration. Commemorating this, all *varkaris* run down this hillock in an unforgettable race in which everyone wins.

Padasparshdarshan and Mookhdarshan

Every devotee can enter the sanctum irrespective of the caste or creed and can even place his head on the feet of the deity by actually touching it. This prized privilege is called *padasparshdarshan* and is exercised by all devotees. For *padsparshadarshan*, it requires 2 to 3 hours on ordinary days, 4 to 5 hours on weekly holidays and *Ekadashi* day and up to 24 to 36 hours on *Yatra* days.

For the devotees who cannot spare long hours in queues for *padsparshadarshan* can have the *mookhdarshan*. In *mookhdarshan*, the *darshan* of Vitthal is taken from the distance of about 25 metres and of Rukmini, from the distance of about 15 metres. It requires only 15 to 20 minutes for such *darshan*.

Darshan in Pandharpur has a distinctive meaning and is valued sentimentally by all the devotees.

SOME OTHER FAMOUS TEMPLES

A Hindu temple is a symbolic representation of God. To Hindus, a temple is the abode of God, hence as sacred as a place of pilgrimage. There are many temples in India. It is not possible to write about all of them in this limited space, so we have taken up here the seven Sun Temples and five other famous temples individually which are like a drop in the vast ocean.

▲ A carving at Mahabalipuram Temple

Seven Sun Temples

Sun Temples or *Aditya Grihas* as they were known in ancient times, have Sun as the presiding deity. Sun has been worshipped in our country since Vedic times.

Five Famous Temples

It is not easy to distinguish a temple from another. We take here five famous temples which are thronged by devotees in large numbers.

Guruvayur Temple in Kerala, **Meenakshi Temple** in Madurai, **Mahabalipuram Temple** in Andhra Pradesh, **Adi Kumbeshwar Temple** in Kumbhakonam and **Kamakshi Amman Temple** in Kanchipuram are some of the famous temples among many others.

▼ The face of Modhera Sun Temple

The Sun as a deity is referred to as *Surya* or *Aditya*. The *Vedas* are full of hymns describing the celestial body as the source and sustainer of all life on earth.

Dakshinaarka Temple in Gaya, **Konark** in Orissa, **Modhera** in Gujarat, **Surya Pahar** in Assam, **Suryanaar Kovil** in Tamil Nadu, **Suryanarayanaswamy** Temple in Arasavilli in Andhra Pradesh, and **Brahmanya Dev Temple** in Unao are some of the well-known Sun Temples in India.

DAKSHINAARKA TEMPLE

The Dakshinaarka Temple in Gaya is an ancient shrine of the Sun God. The worship of Sun in the Magadha region finds its reference in the Puranas and thus this temple is said to be very ancient. Dakshinaarka Temple dates back to the 13th century, when the South Indian emperor Prataparudra of Warangal built it.

▲ A sculpture of Lord Surya

The ritual of offering *pindas* or offerings to the dead has been long associated with Gaya and has been mentioned in the scriptures like *Vayu Purana*. Offerings to the ancestors are made at the **Surya Kund** or the **Dakshina Maanas Kund** in front of the Dakshinaarka Temple.

This temple faces east and it stands close to the **Vishnupada Temple**.

The temple is a simple and plain structure with a dome over it. The comparatively larger *sabha mandap* stands in front of the sanctum. Massive pillars line the *mandap* where graceful stone sculptures of Shiva, Brahma, Vishnu, Surya and Durga can be seen.

There are two other Sun Temples at Gaya, namely the **Uttaraka Temple** near the Uttara Maanas tank and the **Gayaditya Temple** on the river Falgu.

Sun worship was very popular in the Magadha region, which included Gaya. Numerous old images of the Sun God are found in Gaya and there are still quite a number of sun worshippers here. It is said that they may have descended from the fire worshippers of Central Asia. In fact, the granite image of Aditya or the Sun God worshipped here is portrayed as wearing a jacket, a waist girdle and high boots in the Iranian tradition. Hundreds of people visit this temple on Sundays.

▲ A sculpture of Lord Surya

KONARK TEMPLE

*Konark is one of the well-known tourist attractions in Orissa. The name Konark is derived form the words **Kona** which means 'corner' and **Arka**, meaning the Sun. Konark is known for its temple of Lord Surya, the Sun God, situated at the seashore, 33 kilometres from Puri and 64 kilometres from Bhubaneswar. It is constructed of black stone covered with intricately carved sculptures. This temple is considered to be one of the most vivid architectural marvels of India.*

▲ **Lord Surya at Konark**

This temple was built in the 13th century by the Oriya King Raja Narasimhadeva I. It took 1,200 workers over 16 years to build it. The legend of the temple has it that Samba, the son of Krishna, was cursed to suffer from leprosy for 12 years. Since he was cured by Surya, the Sun God, he built a temple dedicated to Surya.

This impressive temple resembles the huge chariot of Sun God with twenty-four huge wheels being pulled by seven horses. Great pairs of large intricately-carved wheels exist on both sides of a 4-metre-high platform on which the temple is erected. There are two rows of twelve wheels on each side of the temple. Some say the wheels represent the twenty-four hours in a day and others say the twelve months. The seven horses are said to symbolise the seven days of the week.

There are three remarkable images of Surya facing different directions to catch the rays of Sun at dawn, noon and dusk. The three statues of Surya change their facial expressions from wakefulness in the morning (south) to weariness towards the end of the day (north).

The main entrance has large statues of two stone lions crushing the elephants.

There is a small shrine dedicated to Mayadevi, the wife of Surya, in the south-west corner of the enclosure. At the northern part of the enclosure, to the right of the entrance, are a group of elephants. At the southern side is a group of horses trampling men.

There is also a temple in the honour of the *Navgrahas* or the nine planets. There is a nice quiet beach at a distance of about 3 kilometres from the temple. Not far from the beach is a pond where Krishna's son Samba is said to have been cured of leprosy.

▲ **Konark Sun Temple representing the chariot of Sun God**

▲ **Wheel at Konark Sun Temple**

▲ **Pillars at Konark Sun Temple**

▲ **Stone work, the upholder of ancient art**

MODHERA TEMPLE

The Sun Temple at Modhera near Ahmedabad in Gujarat was built by King Bhimdev I in 1026. This is a grand temple dedicated to the Sun God. As in the Sun Temple at Konark, this temple was so designed that the rays of the Sun would fall on the image of Surya at the time of the equinoxes.

Even in its ruined state, this Sun Temple stands magnificently. The remains of the temple show how majestic this temple must have been in the past. The *shikhars* are notably absent but the *torans* in the frontal halls, and the intricate carvings in the exterior, certify the splendour of this shrine, which is still home to the Modhera Dance Festival featuring dance celebrities giving exquisite performance in a natural setting. There is no worship offered here now. The temple has a sanctum, a *pradakshina patha* and a *sabha mandap* in front. The exterior of the sanctum has many engraved images of the Sun God, portrayed as wearing a belt and long shoes as in the Dakshinaarka Temple at Gaya.

In front of the temple is a colossal tank, which was once known as **Surya Kund** or **Rama Kund**. The tank has a series of carved steps leading to the bottom. Several miniature shrines adorn the steps of the tank, which is an art gallery in itself.

▼ Surya Kund Tank

▼ The magnificence of Modhera Sun Temple

▼ The hallowed Modhera Sun Temple

◀ Pillars in the temple

SURYA PAHAR TEMPLE

The Surya Pahar Hill in the vicinity of Golapara in Assam is literally an art gallery of Indian sculpture. Ruins of several old temples are scattered all over the hill. This hill is also the seat of a small modern Sun Temple.

▲ Surya Pahar Temple

▲ Lord Surya

Sun worship in Assam, as in other parts of India, dates back to the ancient times. Assam has been referred to as *Pragjyotishapura*. According to the *Kalika Purana*, Brahma created this city as beautiful as Indrapuri, the city of Indra, the king of Gods. The word *Prag* refers to the eastern region, *jyotisha* refers to astrology and *pura* means the city. *Pragjyotishapura* therefore means 'eastern city of astrology'. To the east of Guwahati, there is a hill temple known as **Citrachala**, dedicated to the *Navagraha* or the nine planets.

The **Surya Mandir** on Surya Pahar enshrines a circular sculpture, almost 4 feet in circumference with carved images representing the various celestial bodies including Surya. The centremost figure is surrounded by twelve miniature figures in a seated posture. This figure is that of Sage Kashyapa and the rest of the twelve figures around him are referred to as the twelve Adityas — sons of Kashyapa and Aditi. According to the *Puranas*, the Adityas are twelve in number.

Kalika Purana mentions Surya Pahar as the perpetual abode of the Sun. At the foot of the hill, covering a vast area, are present a good number of Shivalingams cut out of stone.

SURYANAAR TEMPLE

This ancient temple, dedicated to the Sun, is located near Kumbhakonam in Tamil Nadu.

Kumbhakonam and its surroundings abound in huge temples. This well-known temple enshrines the Sun God, Kashi Vishwanath, Vishalakshi and the other eight celestial bodies namely *Chandra* (Moon), *Angarakan* (Mars), *Budha* (Mercury), *Brihaspati* (Jupiter), *Shukra* (Venus), *Shani* (Saturn), *Rahu* and *Ketu*.

In this temple, Surya shares his sanctum with *Brihaspati*, his closest ally. The other seven *grahas* have separate shrines in this complex. This makes the temple unique. Also all the *navagraha* deities here are without their weapons that signifies their most benevolent mood.

An elaborate worship protocol is prescribed for pilgrims visiting here. It starts with worship at the shrine of Ganesha Kol Teertha Vinayaka culminating in circumambulating the temple nine times in an anti-clockwise manner.

In the main sanctum, the deity of Surya is flanked by *Usha* (dawn) and *Chhaya* (shadow).

▲ **A panoramic view**

The tall deity of Surya is in a standing pose holding lotuses in his hands. Outside the temple is a temple tank called **Surya Pushkarni**.

It is believed that those who worship the Sun God and Lord Siva in this temple are blessed with prosperity. Those who are affected by *graha dosham* or by the malefic influence of Shani, Ashtama Shani or Janma Shani also visit this temple for getting relieved of their sufferings. The people suffering from the ill-effects of *kalathara dosham*, *vivaha paribandha dosham*, *putra dosham*, *putra paribandha dosham*, *vidya paribandha dosham* and *udyoga paribandha dosham* are also benefited from worshipping at this temple.

According to *Atharva Veda*, one who worships the Sun God gets relieved from diseases pertaining to the eyes and heart.

▲ Suryanaar Temple

SURYANARAYANASWAMY TEMPLE

▲ **Suryanarayanaswamy Temple**

This is a shrine of the Sun at Arasavalli in Andhra Pradesh. The temple dates back to the 7th century and a Kalinga king is believed to have constructed it. The deity of Surya is 5 feet tall, made of black granite holding lotus buds. The head is crowned by fully spread hood of Adishesha serpent.

In this temple also, the deity is flanked by *Usha* (dawn) and *Chhaya* (shadow) who represent eternity. Padmapani is the name of this Sun God. *Padma* stands for wisdom. This shrine is located near Srikakulam in Andhra Pradesh.

Suryanarayanaswamy Temple is the only Sun Temple where the Sun God is worshipped. People believe that eye and skin diseases

▲ **In the heart of the temple**

are cured through *Surya Namaskars* and forty-two days' worship in this temple. Many people throng to this temple for performing various *pujas*. This temple is known to bring good health and wealth.

This remarkable temple is built in such a way that the early morning sunrays fall on the feet of the deity twice a year, in February and June, even when the five main entrance gates are closed.

The other temples in the complex include the **Shiva Temple**, **Vinayaka Swamy Temple**, **Anjaneya Swamy Temple**, **Kal Bhairava Temple**, **Subrahmanya Swamy Temple** and **Durga Mahalakshmi Temple**.

▲ Shiva temple is a famous temple in the Suryanarayanaswamy complex

BRAHMANYA DEV TEMPLE

The Brahmanya Dev Temple dedicated to the Sun is located at Unao near Jhansi in Madhya Pradesh. The Brahmanya Dev Temple is also known as the Baramju Temple. This temple was patronised by the Peshwas and by the ruler of Datia, which is now the name of a nearby town.

It is a well-visited temple. Local belief is that the worshippers find relief from ailments such as blindness and leprosy and other skin diseases with the blessings of the deity here.

The stone image of the Sun God stands here on a brick platform covered with black plates. Twenty-one triangles representing the twenty-one phases of the Sun are engraved in the shrine. There is a protective brass cover for the image.

Sunday is the special day of worship as it is considered the day of Sun God.

▲ The Surya Yantra

GURUVAYUR TEMPLE

*Guruvayur is a small town in Kerala. A temple dedicated to Lord Krishna is present in this small town famous all over India as a pilgrim centre. This temple is popularly known as Guruvayurappan. This shrine is also called **Dakshina Dwarka** (Dwarka of the South).*

▲ Guruvayurappan

Here is a small idol of Lord Vishnu. This idol is made of black bismuth, a magnetic stone. It represents Mahavishnu carrying his conch, discus, lotus and mace. It is believed that this idol of Vishnu was worshipped by Krishna himself in Dwarka. When Dwarka was flooded, Krishna handed this idol to the Gods, Guru and Vayu, for safekeeping. As they searched for the best place for the idol, they met Parashurama who brought them to Rudrateertha Lake where Shiva sat in meditation. Shiva told them to install the idol on that spot.

Guruvayur is one of the most sacred and important pilgrimage centres in Kerala. The walls of the sanctum sanctorum are inlaid with exquisite mural paintings and carvings. The eastern *nada* is the main entrance to the shrine.

In the *Chuttambalam* (outer enclosure) is a tall gold-plated *Dhwajastambham* (flagpost).

▲ A closer view of Guruvayur Temple

There is also a high *Deepastambham* (pillar of lamps) whose thirteen circular receptacles provide a truly brilliant spectacle, when lit. The square *Sreekovil* is the sacred sanctum sanctorum of the temple which houses the main deity.

Thulabharam or offering a thing equalling your own weight is offered just inside the eastern gate any time after 5 a.m. The temple accepts anything from water to precious gems. The devotees can give anything from bananas, ghee, sugar, jaggery, coconuts to anything unusual they have promised to offer.

The temple celebrates its *utsavam* or annual festival in February/March. The festival begins with elephant race to determine which elephant will raise the flag. It is a spectacular sight.

▼ Guruvayur Temple

MEENAKSHI TEMPLE

▲ Madurai Meenakshi

Madurai is famous as the city of nectar. It is the oldest and second largest city of Tamil Nadu. This city is located on Vaigai River and was the capital of Pandyan rulers. The Pandyan king, Kulasekhara had built a gorgeous temple around which he created a lotus-shaped city. It has been a centre of learning and pilgrimage, for centuries.

The legend says that Indra committed a sin by killing a demon. He wandered the three worlds till he came upon a *swayambhu lingam* under

▲ The gopuram of Meenakshi Temple

▲ Sculpture depicting Meenakshi's marriage

a *kadamba* (oak) tree and worshipped it. His sins forgiven, he built a temple in the honour of Shiva at that spot and covered it with the *vimana* he had brought with himself from the heavens. Centuries later, a merchant passing by found this shrine in this forest. He informed King Kulasekhara Pandyan, who in turn built a city around the temple. A delighted Lord Shiva dropped the divine nectar or *madhu* all over the place to bless the Pandyan king. This gave the city its name 'Madhurapuri' which later came to be known as Madurai.

When the next Pandya, Malayadhwaja, and his queen, Kanchanamala, performed a sacrifice for a child, Lord Shiva made Goddess Parvati step out of the fire as a little girl. She had three breasts. Lord Shiva told the couple that the third breast would disappear when she would set her eyes on the person who was to be her husband. He asked them to name her 'Thadathagai' and bring her up as if she were a boy. She grew up to be a great warrior. She won many wars and ascended the throne after her father. Finally she marched towards Mount Kailash.

When she saw Lord Shiva there, her third breast disappeared. The Lord told her to return to Madurai and said that he would marry her there. The divine marriage was celebrated. Their marriage is the theme used by Madurai artists who have carved superb sculptures in the temple. The crowning of Meenakshi or Thadathagai is celebrated as a festival in the temple.

The Lord performed many miracles at the wedding. These are described in a celebrated poem, the *Tiruviayadal Puranam*. Under the name of Sundara Pandya, Lord Shiva ruled the land with Meenakshi. Later they crowned their son, Lord Murugan and soon after Sundara Pandya and Thadathagai went into the temple and assumed divine forms as Lord Somasundara and Goddess Meenakshi respectively.

In the temple, the divine family — Shiva, Meenakshi, Vinayaka and Subrahmanya (Murugan) — smile down from Rajagopuram as you enter. Ahead is the Ashta Shakti Mandap.

Further ahead is *Meenakshi Naikan Mandap* which has six rows of richly-sculpted pillars and many flower shops. There are *Servaikar Mandap, Thirukalyana Mandap* (the divine wedding hall) and *Mangayarkarasi Mandap* containing many statues.

At the entrance of the 1000-pillared hall, there is a statue of the temple's architect, Ariyanatha Mudaliar.

There are many other *mandaps* like *Mudali Pillai Mandap, Oonjal Mandap* and *Killikondu Mandap*. Crossing the Killikoondu Mandap, you enter the shrine of Goddess Meenakshi whose entrance is guarded by two brass *dwarpalikas*. There are *Maha Mandap, Palli aria* (bedroom of the Goddess and Lord Sundara) and *Artha Mandap*.

The next step is Sundareshwar's Sannidhi. There are two 8-foot-tall images in this place. One is that of Mukkuruni Vinayakar in the outer *prakaram* and the other one is of Nataraja inside the sanctum. Before you exit, there is *Kambathadi Mandap* with sculptures of Shiva and Vishnu in their different manifestations. There is a massive pillar that depicts the divine wedding of Meenakshi and Sundareshwar.

The Lake Potramarai

Potramarai Kulam, the holy pond that measures 165 feet by 120 feet, inside the temple is a very sacred site. The devotees and people go around the lake before entering the main shrine. As per the legend, Lord Shiva promised to a stork that no fish or other marine life would grow here. Hence no marine creatures are found in the lake. In the Tamil myths, the lake is supposed to be a judge for judging a worth of a new literature. Authors place their works here. The poorly written works sink, while the scholarly ones float.

Festivals

A number of festivals are celebrated with great pomp and splendour in this temple. The most important among them is the Meenakshi Thirukalyanam (divine marriage of Meenkashi) that is celebrated in April every year. During this one month period, in which most of the temples in Tamil Nadu celebrate their annual festivals, a number of events including the Ther Thiruvizhah (chariot festival) and Theppa Thiruvizhah (float festival) are held here. Apart from this, major Hindu festivals, like Navaratri and Shivaratri, are also celebrated in a grand manner. Like most Shakti temples in Tamil Nadu, the Fridays during the Tamil months of *Aadi* (July 15 to August 17) and *Thai* (January 15 to February 15) are popularly celebrated with thousands of devotees thronging to the temple.

MAHABALIPURAM TEMPLE

Mahabalipuram is located close to Chennai in Tamil Nadu on the shores of the Bay of Bengal, along the Indian eastern coast. Known for its rock carvings and monolithic sculptures, it has the famous shore temple, the only one to have survived the ravages of nature. It is also known as the Seven Pagodas (temples) but six of them now lie submerged in the sea.

There are two low hills in Mahabalipuram a little away from the sea whose both sides have eleven excavated temples called *mandaps*. Out of a big rock standing free nearby, there is a cut out temple called *ratha*. This type of temple is unique to Mahabalipuram. Built by Narasimha Varman II, who also built the Kailashnath Temple in Kanchipuram, this is one of the earliest structural temples in Tamil Nadu.

▲ Mahabalipuram Temple

▲ Mahabalipuram Lion Pillar

Out of the other hill much smaller and standing towards the south are five more *rathas* and three big sculptures of Nandi, a lion and an elephant. The five *rathas* are of Yudhishthira, Bhima, Arjuna, Draupadi and Sahdeva. Immediately in front of the Draupadi *ratha*, two smaller rocks are sculptured into an elephant and a lion. Behind the Draupadi and Arjuna *ratha* which stand on a common base, there is a sculpture of Nandi.

This Shore Temple occupies a most extraordinary site at the very margin of the Bay of Bengal, so that at high tide the waves sweep into it. For this reason their sculptures have been eroded by the winds and waves of the ocean.

There are three shrines in this temple. Two of them are of Shaiva and the third is of Vaishnava with an image of Lord Anantashayi made of rock. There are *vimanas* over the Shaiva shrines but none over the Vaishnava shrine. They seem to have disappeared with time.

ADI KUMBHESHWAR TEMPLE

Kumbhakonam is known as the town of the celestial pot. From the pilgrim's eyes, this foremost temple town is perhaps the most special destination in the Kaveri Delta.

It is believed that after the deluge and just before the advent of *Kaliyuga* the celestial pot of nectar containing the seeds of life came to rest here. Shiva, in the garb of a hunter, shot an arrow at the pot and broke it making all its contents spill resulting in the revival of life. *Kumbham* means the pot and *konam* means crooked — the pot that broke when Shiva's arrow hit it. Adi Kumbheshwar Temple is dedicated to Lord Shiva who broke the pot and the place where the nectar from the pot fell is called **Mahamaham Tank**.

The four massive towers of the Adi Kumbheshwar Temple are surrounded by high walls. All the *mandaps*, pillars and ceilings of the temple are well sculptured.

Some years ago an underground tunnel was discovered in the temple near the sanctum of Lord Kumbheshwar. The *swayambhu lingam* is slightly lop-sided in shape.

The sanctum of Goddess Mangalambigai is magnificent. The 4-foot-tall idol, sheathed in gold, stands on a gold base. The idol is said to be energised by 72 crore mantras.

Another shrine in the temple complex is that of Jurahareshwar, the God who destroys fever. Devotees pray to him to cure fever.

Mahamaham Tank is close to the Adi Kumbheshwar Temple. It is not a perfect rectangle but it resembles the pot that broke here. There are nineteen *teerthams* (wells) within the tank. On its banks are shrines for sixteen *lingams*.

▼ **Kaveri, Abby Falls**

KAMAKSHI AMMAN TEMPLE

▲ **Goddess Kamakshi Amman**

The Kamakshi Amman Temple at Kanchipuram is an ancient temple and is associated with Adi Shankaracharya. Legend has it that Kamakshi offered worship to a Shivalingam made out of sand under a mango tree and gained Shiva's hand in marriage.

The Kamakshi Amman Temple covers an area of about 5 acres and the sanctum is crowned with a gold plated *vimana*. Kamakshi is enshrined in a seated posture in the sanctum and is referred to as the *Parabrahma Swaroopini*, seated with Brahma, Vishnu and Sadashiva.

It is believed that Kamakshi was originally an *Ugra Swaroopini*, and that Adi Shankaracharya, upon establishing the Shri Yantra, personified her as the *Shanta Swaroopini*. It is believed that during the days of Adi Shankara, the presence of the *Ugra Swaroopini* was felt outside the temple precincts and that Shankaracharya had requested her not to leave the temple complex.

The outer *prakaram* houses the temple tank and several *mandaps* including the 100-pillared hall. Imposing views of the golden *vimana* can be had from the outer *prakaram*, which has four entrances on the four sides. Images of Vishnu can also be seen near the temple tank.

One first enters the four-pillared hall and then the inner *prakaram*.

▲ **The chariot festival**

▲ **Kamakshi Amman Temple**

Thereafter, one climbs a series of steps to reach the sanctum. Immediately surrounding the sanctum are small shrines of Ardhanareshwar, Soundaryalakshmi, Kalvar and Varaahi. In this *prakaram*, the shrines of Bangaru Kamakshi, Mahasaraswati and Adi Shankaracharya are present.

Kanchipuram is the seat of the Kanchi Kamakoti Peetham established by Adi Shankaracharya. It is believed that Shankaracharya attained *samadhi* at Kanchipuram, although another school of thought holds that Kedarnath in the Himalayas is the site of his *samadhi*.

Four worship services are offered each day here. The jewels adorning the image of the deity are of great beauty. The annual festival *Brahmotsavam* is celebrated for 13 days. The silver chariot festival falls on the 7th day. Other festivals include Navaratri, Aadi and Aippasi Pooram, Shankara Jayanti and Vasanta Utsavam.

A LIST OF OTHER IMPORTANT AND POPULAR TEMPLES IN INDIA

1. **Achaleshwar Mahadeo Temple at Achalgarh near Mount Abu in Rajasthan**
Shiva Temple featuring an image of the toe of Shiva and a brass Nandi

2. **Adhar Devi Temple at Mount Abu in Rajasthan**
Durga Temple in rock cleft near Mount Abu

3. **Amba Mata Temple at Junagarh in Gujarat**
Located on top of the 600-metre-high Girnar Hill

4. **Ambika Mata Temple at Jagat near Udaipur in Rajasthan**
10th century temple dedicated to Ambika

5. **Arbada Mata Temple at Eklingji near Udaipur in Rajasthan**
Located in Eklingji, home to the famous Eklingji Temple

6. **Atri Rishi Temple at Guru Shikhar near Mount Abu in Rajasthan**
On top of the 5300-foot-high hill, the Guru Shikhar, the loftiest point in Rajasthan

7. **Balaji Temple at Bharatpur near Jaipur in Rajasthan**

8. **Baroli Temple at Baroli near Kota in Rajasthan**
One of the oldest temple complexes (9th century AD) in Rajasthan

9. **Brahma Temple at Pushkar near Ajmer in Rajasthan**
Only one of its kinds, Brahma Temple with a red spire

10. **Bhrigu Rishi Temple at Broach in Gujarat**
City name Bharuch derived from Bhrigukachba after this temple

11. **Bijolia Temple at Bijolia near Bundi in Rajasthan**
A complex of ancient temples once numbering hundred, now just three

12. **Chamunda Temple at Jodhpur in Rajasthan**
Durga Temple located in the Meherangarh Fort in Jodhpur

13. **Chintamani Temple at Bikaner in Rajasthan**
Part of the Bhand Sagar Temple complex

14. **Durgiana Temple at Amritsar in Punjab**
16th century Durga Temple

15. **Dwarkadhish Temple at Kankroli near Udaipur in Rajasthan**
Similar to the Nathdwara Temple at Nathdwara

16. **Dwarkanath Temple at Dwarka in Gujarat**
One of the holiest Hindu temples dedicated to Krishna with a 5-storey spire and 60 columns

17. **Eklingji Temple at Eklingji near Udaipur in Rajasthan**
Ornate 8th century Shiva Temple with beautiful pillars

18. **Gaumukh Temple near Mount Abu in Rajasthan**
Associated with the mythological sage Vasistha

19. **Gopinath Temple at Bhangarh near Alwar in Rajasthan**
Abandoned beautiful yellow stone carved temple on a 14-foot-high platform, with intricate sculptural work

20. **Hanuman Temple at Bhangarh near Alwar in Rajasthan**

21. **Har Mandir Shiva Temple at Bikaner in Rajasthan**
Located in the Junagarh Fort at Bikaner

22. **Harshat Mata Temple at Abhaneri near Jaipur in Rajasthan**
Known for sculptural remains of the post Gupta Period monuments of the 9th century AD

23. **Jagdish Temple at Udaipur in Rajasthan**
Grand 17th century temple to Vishnu located near Udaipur city palace

24. **Jaisalmer Shiva Temple at Jaisalmer in Rajasthan**
Located in the Jaisalmer Fort along with a Ganesh Temple

25. **Kailashpuri Temple Ruins at Eklingji near Udaipur in Rajasthan**
Ruins of Shiva and Vishnu Temples in Eklingji known for the Eklingji Temple

26. **Kali Temple at Amber near Jaipur in Rajasthan**
Temple located in the fortress palace in Ambar (16th century AD)

27. **Kalika Mata Temple at Chittorgarh in Rajasthan**
An 8th century Sun Temple converted to Kali Temple in the Chittorgarh Fort near the Padmini Palace

28. **Karni Mata Temple at Deshnok near Bikaner in Rajasthan**
Marble carvings and a silver door adorn this temple where rats are cared for

29. **Kiradu Temples at Kiradu near Barmer in Rajasthan**
11th century Kathiawar style temples with Gupta elements

30. **Krishna Temple at Jaisalmer in Rajasthan**
Temple near the arched gateway to the Gadi Sagar Water Tank

31. **Krishna Temples at Bet Island near Dwarka in Gujarat**
Modern Krishna Temples in this island near Dwarka

32. **Kumbha Shyam Temple at Chittorgarh in Rajasthan**
Large Temple in the Chittorgarh Fort

33. **Laxmi Narayan Temple at Amritsar in Punjab**
Laxmi and Narayan Temple built in the middle of a lake

34. **Mahamandir Shiva Temple at Mahamandir near Jodhpur in Rajasthan**
A 100-pillared Shiva Temple

35. **Mallinath Temple at Junagarh in Gujarat**
Marble Temple on Girnar Hill along with 4 other Jain Temples dating back to the 12th century

36. **Mata Bhavani Temple at Ahmedabad in Gujarat**
Associated with the Mat Bhavani step well

37. **Meera Temple at Chittorgarh in Rajasthan**
Ornate temple in the Chittorgarh Fort

38. **Menal Shiva Temples at Menal near Bundi in Rajasthan**
A complex of Shiva Temples from the Gupta Period

39. **Nathdwara at Nathdwara near Udaipur in Rajasthan**
19th century temple bearing image of Vishnu brought from Mathura in the 17th century

40. **Neelkanth Mahadev Temple at Chittorgarh in Rajasthan**
Temple located near Padmini's palace of the Chittorgarh Fort

41. **Ramgarh Temples at Ramgarh near Kota in Rajasthan**
Accessible by jeep

42. **Ranchodrai Temple at Dakor near Baroda in Gujarat**
Krishna Temple famous for the Sharad Purnima festival in October/November

43. **Rangji Temple at Pushkar near Ajmer in Rajasthan**
An important temple in the temple town of Pushkar

44. **Rathasan Devi Temple at Eklingji near Udaipur in Rajasthan**
Rashtrasena Devi Temple in Eklingji known for the famous Eklingji Temple

45. **Sammidheshwar Temple at Chittorgarh in Rajasthan**
Temples located in the Rana Kumbha Palace of the Chittorgarh Fort

46. **Sas Bahu Temple at Eklingji near Udaipur in Rajasthan**
A complex of temples with fine carvings, dating back to the 11th century

47. **Sharda Pith Temple at Pilani in Rajasthan**
Modern marble temple of learning at the Birla Institute of Technology and Science

48. **Shiva Temple at Chittorgarh in Rajasthan**
Temple located in the Rana Kumbha Palace of the Chittorgarh Fort

49. **Sidhpur Temple Ruins at Sidhpur near Ahmedabad in Gujarat**
Near the Mehsana the drop-off point for Modhera

50. **Sila Devi (White Marble) Temple at Amber near Jaipur in Rajasthan**
Temple located in the fortress palace in Amber (16th century AD)

51. **Sirsa Mata Temple at Bhangarh near Alwar in Rajasthan**

52. **Someshwar Mahadev Temple at Bhangarh near Alwar in Rajasthan**
Shiva Temple with a great lingam (marble) in the abandoned Rajput settlement

53. **Somanth Temple at Somnath Patan near Veraval in Gujarat**
One of the 12 Jyotirlingams in India, and an ancient temple, current structure belongs to this century

54. **Soyalla Shiva Temple at Soyala near Jodhpur in Rajasthan**
75 kilometres from Jodhpur on the Nagpur Road

55. **Sun Temple at Ranakpur near Udaipur in Rajasthan**
Temple is located in the Ranakpur Temple complex

56. **Sun Temple at Galta near Jaipur in Rajasthan**
A temple built on a hill dedicated to Surya

57. **Sun Temple at Modhera near Ahmedabad in Gujarat**
Ruins of well-known 11th century temple intricately sculpted

58. **Sun Temple at Somnath Patan near Veraval in Gujarat**
Ancient temple with interesting sculpture dating back to the period of the Somnath Temple, near a rebuilt Somnath Temple of the Ahilyabai Holkar period

59. **Surya (Sun) Temple at Jhaira Patan near Kota in Rajasthan**
Ruins of an ancient temple

60. **Swami Narayan Temple at Ahmedabad in Gujarat**
19th century temple enclosed in a large courtyard

61. **Takteshwar Temple at Bhavnagar in Gujarat**
Hilltop temple with great views

62. **Vindhyavasani Devi Temple at Eklingji near Udaipur in Rajasthan**
Located in Eklingji known for its famous Eklingji Temple

63. **Asvakranta Temple at Guwahati in Assam**
Temple with interesting carvings enshrines a reclining image of Vishnu of great workmanship

64. **Barpeta Satra at Barpeta near Guwahati in Assam**
This Vaishnavite congregational site is decorated with finely engraved and painted wooden panels and ceilings

65. **Dah Parbatiya Temple at Tezpur in Assam**
Ruins of the oldest and finest piece of architectural work in Assam

66. **Devi Dol at Gaurisagar near Golaghat in Assam**
This is a temple dedicated to Devi with interesting architectural and sculptural features

67. **Devi Temple at Shibsagar in Assam**
A large temple dedicated to Devi on the banks of Shibsagar Tank

68. **Govindaji Temple at Imphal in Manipur**

69. **Hatimura Temple at silghat in Assam**
Mahisamardini Temple, an important centre of Shakti worship, a brick temple built over old stone temple ruins (17th century)

70. **Hayagriva Mahadeva Temple at Hajo near Guwahati in Assam**
An imposing temple with a shikhara and interesting sculptural work where the presiding deity is worshipped as the Man Lion incarnation of Vishnu by the Hindus and as Buddha by Buddhists (ancient temple rebuilt in the 16th century)

71. **Kamakhya Temple at Guwahati in Assam**
A centre for Shakti worship (a peetha) rebuilt in the 16th century – on Neelanchal Hill and is a good specimen of Assamese sculptural work

72. **Kedareshwara Temple at Hajo near Guwahati in Assam**

73. **Navagraha Temple at Guwahati in Assam**
Located on Chitrachal Hill and once a centre for the study of astrology this temple dates back to the 17th century

74. **Negriting Temple at Shibsagar in Assam**
Shiva Temple dating back to the 17th century rebuilt on a hill in the 18th century – a grand temple with beautiful sculptural work

75. **Sib Dol Temple at Shibsagar in Assam**
This Shiva Temple on the banks of the Shibsagar Tank is an important landmark in the artistic history of Assam

76. **Sukreshwara Temple at Guwahati in Assam**
Said to be worshipped by Sage Sukra, this 18th century temple is believed to have the largest *lingam* in India

77. **Sun Temple at Gopalpura in Assam**
A relatively modern temple enshrines a circular stone tablet with 12 Adityas with Kashyapa in the centre; the Surya Pahar Hill is virtually a picture gallery of archaeological remains

78. **Tamreshwari Temple at Sadiya in Assam**
Ruins of this temple represent one of the oldest and most important temples in the region – a centre of tantric worship

79. **Ugra Tara Temple at Guwahati in Assam**
This important Shakti shrine dates back to the 18th century

80. **Umananda Temple at Guwahati in Assam**
Located on Peacock Island in the middle of a river accessible by ferry this 17th century temple (later rebuilt) has some fine rock-cut figures

81. **Vasishtashrama Temple at Guwahati in Assam**
The Shiva Temple in Vasishtashrama is the last Ahom monument in the Guwahati region (18th century)

82. **Vishnu Temple at Shibsagar in Assam**
A three acre temple dedicated to Vishnu on the banks of the Shibsagar Tank

OTHER HINDOOLOGY BOOKS

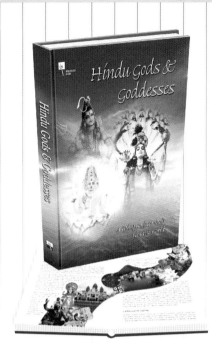

Rs. 499/- • Colour (H.B.)
Code: 9983 D • pp: 174 • Size: 8.5" x 11"

Rs. 399/- • Colour (H.B.)
Code: 9984 E • pp: 96 • Size: 8.5" x 11"

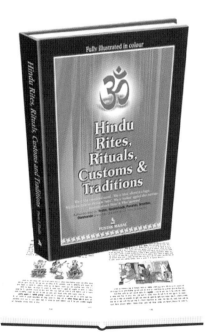

Rs. 199/- • Colour (H.B.)
Code: 4128 D • pp: 328 • Size: 7.25" x 9.5"

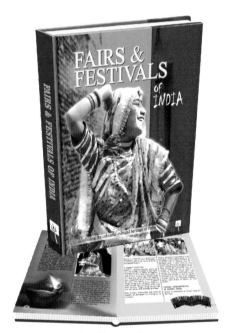

Rs. 399/- • Colour (H.B.)
Code: 4151 A • pp: 148 • Size: 8" x 10"

'Hindoology Books', our new imprint, is dedicated to exploring Hinduism and enlightening our readers about the various remarkable aspects of this religion. The books published under this imprint are enriched with vivid pictures and exclusively designed to surpass the highest standards of content and production, which make them a true value for money. *Hindu Pilgrimages* is one of our forthcoming books, which would take you on a mental journey to various spiritual places of the country. With your support and overwhelming response from the world over, we plan to publish more such titles under this imprint.

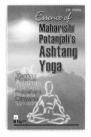

4133 A • Rs. 60/-

9989 D • Rs. 96/-

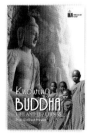

4152 B • Rs. 96/-

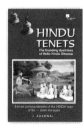

9987 E • Rs. 150/-

4131 C • Rs. 50/-

4116 B • Rs. 80/-

9988 C • Rs. 60/-